Never Too Late

Mary McDowell

Harvest House Publishers
Eugene, Oregon 94702

Never Too Late
Copyright ©1981 by Mary McDowell
Published by Harvest House Publishers, Eugene, Oregon 97402
Library of Congress Catalog Card Number 82-082811
ISBN 0-89081-365-5

Printed in the United States of America.

I dedicate this book

To God, who gave me the love for people and the desire to help them;

To my son, Dr. Connally Evans, his two sons, Chris and Eric, and daughter, Melanie Summey, whose very existence made me want to be a success in order that they would be proud to call me Mother and Grandmother;

To Mary Kay Ash, founder of Mary Kay Cosmetics, and Gerald Allen, who gave me the opportunity of a Mary Kay career;

To the staff of the Mary Kay Company, who have been so kind to help me these years;

To all the beautiful directors and consultants in the Mary Kay Company;

To Fay Connell, who created in me the desire to write about my experiences; and

To Lucille Rogers and Juanita Dodson, who typed the manuscript.

Contents

Contents

PREFACE

The purpose of this book is to try to explain to the many Mary Kay directors and beauty consultants across these United States—as well as friends and others who may be interested—how I have earned over $400,000 since beginning a new career after I was sixty-three years old.

Also since I started selling beauty products for Mary Kay, how I have been able to be in Queens Court eleven straight years for either selling or recruiting and was Queen one year for Director of Personal Sales and Queen of Recruiting one year—all in a small town in West Texas of 9,000 people!

In January, 1981 just after the annual Dallas seminar for Mary Kay consultants, all of a sudden I realized what God and Mary Kay Cosmetics had done for me.

On that Sunday morning I drove up to the door of my church, suddenly remembering the first time I entered that same door in 1952. I was a new widow with no credit, in a strange town, didn't drive a car, could not type one word on a typewriter, never had used a filing cabinet, and didn't know where the next meal was coming from. I had only forty dollars to my name. That morning I left my purse in the choir room and someone stole my forty dollars!

I was wearing my precious little ring that my preacher-husband had given me, which had a diamond so small one could hardly see it. And here I was twenty-five years later entering that same door after driving up in a $15,300 Cadillac, wearing a $5,000 mink coat. On my dress was a pin and diamonds worth $7,800 plus a valuable wristwatch on my arm, all of which were gifts and prizes given me by Mary Kay Cosmetics.

Then I remembered my $100,000 home I had just left, paid for in full with Mary Kay money I had earned. In this home I had $64,000 worth of antiques, $34,000 worth of silver and $3,000 worth of hand-painted china, all paid for with Mary Kay money.

When all these thoughts flooded my mind, I opened the door and there stood my preacher in the entrance hall. I reached out my hand and said, "Preacher, I just want to tell you what God has done for me. Twenty-five years ago I walked through that door not knowing where the next meal was coming from. The first money I earned out here was from making flowers from discarded ladies' hose and screen wire which I sold to friends. Now see what God has done for me! Mary Kay Ash gave me the opportunity and God led me step by step and just see what good has come to me."

This book is my effort to help every girl have the same life and success I have. The principles and techniques would probably be just as valuable in other fields, I would imagine, because it is God first, others second, and yourself last.

A final thing I want to say is that the people I have met and associated with through the company outweigh all the financial gains. If I had not made one dollar, learning to discipline myself to achieve and to love would have been worth it all.

Grab this opportunity and run with it. So many of you have youth, health, and beauty. Don't waste it. Turn it into a beautiful life.

—Mary McDowell

Never Too Late

Mary McDowell

CHAPTER I

WHY NOT ME?

My Mary Kay career started in 1967 with a phone call. I had just passed my sixty-third birthday.

I had been married to Mr. C. H. McDowell four years. Those four years had been wonderful years in my life. I had no financial fears because Mr. McDowell had been a teacher at A. & M. College for thirty-seven years before our marriage and was now retired. He and his first wife had saved his money through these years and, as he always said, lived frugally.

So I had no money worries but I became restless for need of something to do. One day a Mrs. Jewell Jackson called me and asked me if I knew of anyone whom her daughter might get to sell Mary Kay Cosmetics.

I should explain that at that point in my life I was a professional joiner. I belonged to the church, taught a large Sunday school class, organized an American Business Women's Association chapter with 125 members, was a member of a garden club, member of two dinner clubs, the Eastern Star, had been one of the organizers of a Y.W.C.A. for Odessa, and had been president of City Service Council for two years. In fact, I found myself running from one meeting, almost breaking the speed limit to get to another. I was spending the greater part of my husband's income on dues, meals, and gifts.

Knowing this about me, Mrs. Jackson thought I could find someone to sell Mary Kay for her daughter. She opened the conversation by telling me what a great company Mary Kay was, about how Mary Kay started the company, and about her philosophy of God first, family second, and business third. Then she told me about the product and how great it was, how it would make older people look younger, remove scars, and many, many other things about the product. She gave such glowing explanations of how it had changed people who used in consistently, and continued with many beautiful fascinating things about what it could do for its users.

Then she told me about how everyone in the company loved each other. She then went on to tell me how much money one could make. She was talking so fast, I didn't have time to think.

Mrs. Jackson then told me that her daughter had been with Commercial College in Dallas for six years previously and that her salary there had been $700 per month. This really got my attention, for $700 per month in 1967 sounded almost unbelievable to me. She said her daughter had quit this good-paying job to begin selling Mary Kay and was doing even better for them than she had previously. I knew Mrs. Jackson to be a truthful woman and I believed her but I was astonished.

When she finally ran down in her glowing remarks, I said, "Why not me?" She says to this day that she almost fell on the floor when I said those words. I was the last person on earth she thought would sell cosmetics. She then said, "Could you have a show in the morning?" It was then nine in the evening. I stammered out, ". . . In the morning?" She said, "Oh you need only six people." So the time was set for ten o'clock the next morning.

Who in the world could I call at nine in the evening to come to a beauty show at ten the next morning? I started thinking fast. I had two good friends I could call on anytime for anything so I called them. They both accepted the invitation. This made three people including me.

Nine o'clock sharp the next day Mrs. Jackson's daughter was ready to put on the show. Her name was Maxine Rieckert and she was loaded with materials. I began to wonder if she had decided to move in with me, she had so much makeup with her. She had six complete sets in one big laundry basket. Another laundry basket had product trays, another overnight bag with sales aids, a tablecloth and a centerpiece for the table. So you can imagine how much she had brought to hold a show, and I had only three persons including myself!

I had just recently bought a full supply of Brand X cosmetics that cost me much more than the price of Mary Kay's. Maxine went to work setting the table, arranging everything.

She then started the show. She talked to us and worked with us for three hours. When she closed her show and took the orders, she had sold eighty-four dollars worth of products, and secretly I felt this was a lot of money for her to get in three hours. Forty dollars was her profit. Just think, forty dollars. That was a lot, I thought.

After the show, I filled out the beauty case agreement, paid her for it, and told her I wanted to find out some more about the product before I bought my order. Little did Maxine know when I filled out this agreement with her name on it that she would receive many, many hundreds of dollars from that one recruit. One month, I remember, after she quit selling and was put into my unit, I mailed her a $250 check on my orders alone for that month.

Maxine explained to me that I would need to place a $250 order for my product to sell. This was the minimum at that time in order to make a fifty percent profit on the product. And since I was going to sell, I didn't want to miss the profit of fifty percent. (Incidentally, I have been with the company over fourteen years now and never have I placed one single order under the minimum.)

Since most people in my town knew me, I wanted to make sure the product I was going to sell was everything I had heard it was. I certainly could not go around saying something was good when it was not. My image was at stake. So I decided to go to Dallas and spend one week with Maxine, the lady who sponsored me. I wanted to learn all about the product.

On Monday morning I was in the Mary Kay office to attend a sales meeting. Anna Ewing conducted the meeting. I met Mary Kay and the office staff after the meeting was over.

Susie Vickers had recruited Maxine and she was on hand to see we were shown around. She arranged for me to come to her house and she put on a show just for me. Some more of the consultants set up and went through a show just for my benefit. By the end of the week, I was thoroughly convinced that all I had been told about Mary Kay was true. I placed my order and returned home.

All the way home I wrote down names of friends I would call and invite to my home for a facial. After I arrived home, the next day I began my Mary Kay career. I picked up my list and started to call everyone on that list. But I never dialed a single one on the phone. The very first name I eliminated. I thought, "Oh, she won't buy anything." I covered the whole list and crossed every name out making excuses for every one on the list.

I had to get some people for my show someplace, so I started another list. I first invited six people to my home. This made a show, and I did really well. So from there I started setting up shows with friends. By this time some of the people I had eliminated from my first list would say to me, "Guess what? I have just bought that beautiful Mary Kay you are selling and I love it." I would burn with jealousy. But I learned a great lesson: I learned never to eliminate a single person once I thought of someone.

I faced many disappointments at first because I expected all my friends to come rushing in to buy my product, and certainly I expected my family to do so. But they didn't. I could not understand why my dearest friends and my family didn't buy from me.

I had worked for the Baptist church eight years, had worked with all the youth groups, held Vacation Bible Schools, arranged weddings, and done so much for so many people, and I felt hurt when they bought their product from someone else.

Finally I became reconciled to the fact that your friends feel you are making something off them; therefore, they would rather buy from someone else. When I learned this, I turned to people I didn't know and did so much better. My first month, I earned a golden goblet and a Polaroid camera for a $1,000 order.

The Mary Kay Company had at that time what was known as the Golden Goblet Club. During the time that they had this, I earned 46 Golden Goblets. At that time I still didn't intend to sell Mary Kay cosmetics very long. I had a wonderful time, but I didn't know why.

By the end of the year, my husband, Mr. McDowell, had contracted cancer which was too far advanced when the doctors found it. He was sent home to live as long as he could because there was nothing they could do for him. He lived three months longer. Those were trying days for me. My selling slowed down due to my responsibilities to my husband.

The annual Mary Kay seminar in Dallas was coming up just a few days after my husband's death. My son and his family were in town for the funeral and were spending a few days with me to help me get settled down after my husband's death. He knew how much I wanted to go to the seminar. He arranged, without my knowing it, for some of my friends to buy me the prettiest gown they could find, and he demanded that I go to the seminar.

I didn't want to go to the seminar after the experience of my husband's death, but my son made a proposition: If I would go, they would get a hotel or motel close by the Marriott where the seminar was to be held and stay there to be near me. This sounded like a good arrangement, so I accepted it. We all took off for Dallas, and I went to the seminar.

I do believe attending this seminar was the most exciting experience I have ever had in my whole life. Mary Kay laid down the red carpet, literally. (There was red carpet in the aisles of the hall where we met.) At the entrance we had escorts dressed in tuxedos for all the consultants who didn't have a husband. She gave every consultant a beautiful orchid and Mary Kay presented a gold goblet to each gal who had earned one. The music was playing and the excitement was tremendous. The next day the seminar got in full swing. Everyone was hilariously happy. The directors that year wore gold western-type suits with big western hats.

Our own darling Susie Vickers was running around doing all sorts of funny things, and she had on one of those gold suits. Something happened to me that day that I can't explain. But all of a sudden, I decided I would become a director.

My son had been trying to get me to retire for sometime, but I had refused. All of a sudden the thought came to me: I am going to make director just to prove to my family that I was not ready to be put on the shelf. I would show them I could compete with young women with more education than I. Then when I had done that, I could quit. I had no idea I would still be selling fourteen years later.

I developed a burning desire to go to the top just for my family. In my way of thinking at that point in my life, I thought I would rather be a director than president of the United States.

I came home determined to make director. I started booking shows selling $500 and $600 per week. I started recruiting. I held as many as three shows per day.

I always attended sales meetings. Somehow I developed the feeling my director didn't want me to make director. So I slowed down. In fact, one day I told myself this was my last sales meeting. But something was said or done that day that made me want more than ever to make director.

Plus there was Maxine. She tried so hard to train us right. She went on and made director. Now we had a director here in our town. This made us very happy. She was everything a director should be—in looks and ability. She worked so hard at her job.

At this time we had to order each month or be terminated. When I would get up to seven or eight recruits, someone in the group would be terminated. I didn't know how to recruit very well, and I would have a setback. I finally had nine recruits.

All of a sudden I realized I was going to be working

with younger and prettier women. But I saw this only as a challenge, not a deterrent, and I accepted the challenge to succeed. I threw myself into my work and loved every minute of it. I met new people and broadened my horizons.

The second year in Mary Kay Company I was recognized for being the top salesperson in my unit. We came to our yearly meeting in Dallas, Texas, and I was presented to 2,100 people as being the Queen of Sales in my unit. This was very good for my ego.

Next year I was fifth in sales for the whole nationwide company. Again I was presented on stage and received a fine watch. The following year I was given a diamond brooch and was third from the top in sales. Then the next year I was second and all this time my sales were increasing, so this meant more money for me.

After the second year, I earned the place of Director and during the fourth year, I was named Senior Director with another director under me.

During the year of my seventy-fifth birthday, I was selected from 47,000 persons as number one in recruiting in the nation.

I bought a $60,000 home and was able to pay off the mortgage in 1980. My earnings in 1980 totaled $36,000, or $3,000 every month, and I am now over seventy-seven years old!

Besides the money I make, I have won many valuable prizes from the company, including a pink Cadillac, a new Buick, plus many items of beautiful jewelry and prizes for the home. All of these gifts were premiums earned for my sales production.

I photocopied the first $6,000 check I received and sent it to my son, who had moved away from West Texas. I did the same with my first $2,000, $3,000, and $4,000 checks. Every time I would ask him, "Did you ever think your mother would make so much money in her retirement years?"

Proud of myself? You bet! I am happy and satisfied too. I have proven that people are only as old as they think. Today I have found a wonderful new life for myself. I have my own identity.

I have asked myself thousands of times why I said, "Why not me?" when Jewell Jackson called me that day and said, "Can you find me someone who would be willing to sell Mary Kay?"

Now I know perfectly well why I said those words. It is all so clear now. You see, I am a born-again Christian. Being born again means one day I accepted Jesus Christ as my Savior and when I did, I became his child. In I Corinthians 2:16, it says, "We have a portion of the very mind of Christ." This being so, He led me that day to say, "Why not me?" I had no idea that my whole life would be molded into this company I now represent.

At that point in my life, I was struggling to find my own identity. I had been a preacher's wife for thirty-two years. All those years I was the preacher's wife. After his death, for eight years I was on the staff of Belmont Baptist Church where my son was the pastor. Those years I was the preacher's mother. My son's name is Connally Evans, and many invitations I received for wedding showers, graduations and so on, were addressed to me as Mrs. D. Connally Evans. This made me want to have my own identity.

Also, we had many people going from door to door selling cosmetics, some looking more like housemaids than cosmetic representatives. So I knew I had to change that image. Many times in my rushed way of life, I would get up in the morning and not fix my face, comb my hair, or dress until noon. Many times I would run out to the nearby grocery not dressed like a professional lady. This I would have to change.

Most of all I knew that I would have to represent a company that was honest and the product had to be good. The chairman of the board and founder of the company, Mary Kay Ash, and I have been closely associated these many years. And without a doubt, she is the greatest person I have ever met or known. You will find her to be the most knowledgeable person you can find. She really knows people inside and out. Don't ever allow yourself for one minute to believe you can pull anything over her and she not know it. She may allow you to believe she does not know it, but she does. She will come up with the right answer ever time. Whenever I have a problem of any kind, I will call her and she will help to solve it. And she is never too busy to listen to you. She has a heart full of love for everyone and makes each one of us feel we are her favorites.

She will listen to you when you need her. Never be afraid to approach her anytime. She has seen that every member of her staff is the same way. I wish the world all over could have the love the Mary Kay Company has.

Mary Kay has provided every single thing in the world that she could find to help us do our work more efficiently. We have a special person in our company for everything. They are there to help us. We are provided with all the materials that we need to help us present our product in a special way.

I learned our product is special. It is not like ordinary products. We never have to apologize for our product. We can present it with pride in a professional way. Mary Kay has given us a special image to carry with us.

CHAPTER II

LIVING WITH SELF

Self-determination

Winners make it happen; losers let it happen.

The true meaning of self-control is often misunderstood. Many people interpret self-control as getting a good grip on yourself, or remaining calm, cool, and passive under pressure. Self-control as it relates to the psychology of winning is synonymous to self-determination.

To be a winner in life we must take full responsibility for determining our actions in our lives. We must believe and have as our philosophy that life is a do-it-yourself program.

This is your business. No one will do it for you. We shape our own destiny. There is no such thing as luck or fate to make you a winner. No assurance that you will be a success. You make your own success. You are what you are as a result of your own doings. Whether you were born on the back side of nowhere, skid row, or on the best street in any town, you can pat yourself on the back and say I am totally to blame for what I am today. You and you alone are behind the wheel in your life.

There are some questions you should ask yourself: Are you steering your own ship? Or do you depend on someone else to steer it for you? Do you depend on fate to take you on your journey of life? Are you a puppet dangling from a string of your heredity or your environment? Do you allow things to force you into defeat?

You need not be hung up on the past. You have today and tomorrow and the next. These, too, will pass into yesterdays. So make the best of them today.

Don't leave your self-development to chance. Grab the stairway of life and swing into the future, joyful, happy, because you have developed self-control.

This is being true to yourself—taking control, accepting responsibility. In the final analysis, we are the only ones from whom we can steal time, talent, and accomplishments. We are the only true judges in our own daily life.

Make up your mind. Tell yourself you do not choose to be a common everyday person. It is your right in life to be uncommon if you want to. Tell yourself you are seeking opportunity, not security. You don't want to be a kept citizen, humbled and dulled by having the state look after you.

Spend your time winning. You have no time to lose. Tell yourself you deserve a beautiful life and you are going after it—today, not tomorrow.

Living Examples

We must be willing to be an example for good to our customers and, if we are a director, to our consultants. That is, if we have something in our lives we think is not bad, but someone else does, we must be willing to separate ourselves from that something for their sake. You see, they expect us to be above the average. Let me tell you a story that will illustrate this.

During World War II, about 1944, my husband was a Baptist minister and was called to preach in a small farming community near the town of Moshiem, Tennessee.

The church was small and the members felt they could not pay a very high salary. They loved us and wanted to give us a good place to live. So they found a beautiful big house with three acres of land in the yard. It had a garden plus a beautiful barn that was as pretty as the house.

In back of the house there was a huge grapevine, some peach trees, and the most fertile land that could ever be found. We grew tomatoes the size of dinner plates! The members boasted they had the most beautiful parsonage in the whole state of Tennessee. We were so proud of our new home.

We bought a cow to furnish milk and butter, a hog to kill for our winter's meat, and the church had a beef killed for our freezer. My job was to can all the food we needed. I had learned to can from my mother and I delighted in canning everything I could get.

Time came for the grapes to ripen and the big vine was loaded with big beautiful blue grapes. One bunch would weigh at least two pounds, it was so heavily laden. I was so greedy since I had never had grapes of my own in my whole life. I began to think: What can I do with all these grapes? Of course, there was no sale for them since about everyone in the community had their own. One day a friend told me I could make some grape juice with them. She said the easy way to do it was to put one pint of grapes in a half-gallon canning jar, add one pint of sugar, and fill the jar to the top with boiling water. This sounded wonderful. I picked the grapes, washed them, and put them in jars. When I finished counting, I had twenty gallons of grape juice in the making. Now sugar had been rationed during the war, so I thought, "That sure is a lot of sugar!" But I assured myself that the grape juice would be worth it.

We had a big basement with a concrete wall three feet high all the way around the basement. This provided such a nice place for storing the canned goods. I carried all the jars of grapes down to the basement and left them. What my friend had failed to tell me was that I should not move the jars after they had been filled, for if I did they would turn to wine.

My attention was directed to different activities of the church and I forgot my grapes. There came a day when I went to the basement for something and my precious grapes had spewed out of the jars and run down the sides of the containers. I was greatly distressed. "There goes my precious sugar," I said to myself. I tasted the juice; it tasted delicious. But it was not grape juice and I knew it. I kept trying to rationalize with myself saying this couldn't be wine and that I just could not destroy all that precious sugar. I went back upstairs with a troubled mind. What was I to do?

At this time I was teaching a Sunday school class and can you believe it, the lesson that Sunday was on temperance. Being a teetotaler, I was really having a problem for I still kept telling myself, surely I had not made wine. With my mind in conflict Sunday morning, I went to the dictionary to see what the meaning of wine was. Now I knew what wine was, but I still wanted convincing that what I had down in the basement was not wine. The definition I found stood out in bold letters: fermented grapes. Then I knew I could not teach a temperance lesson with twenty gallons of wine in my basement! I couldn't do this to my preacher-husband. Down the stairs I dashed, carried it all out to the hog trough and gave it to that 400-pound hog.

We rushed off to Sunday school. I taught my lesson, my husband preached, and we came back home. After Sunday dinner, my husband went to the barn and came back laughing hilariously. He told me he had seen our beautiful big hog so drunk it had trouble getting out of the barn with its big doors. He would start for the door and run into the wall and go, "Ugh, ugh," then go to the other side and run into the wall there. Finally it got out, crawled under one of the peach trees and lay there three days until it sobered up.

Needless to say I took lots of ribbing, such as, "So the preacher's wife gets her hogs drunk." I did have a clear conscience teaching my Sunday school class, but I could have kept the wine and drunk it and even enjoyed it, for I'd like to taste good wine. My friends and neighbors would not have known it. But I would have known it and my husband would have known it. Therefore my teaching would have been lifeless, without power.

I remembered what Paul said to the Corinthian Christians in I Corinthians 8:12, 13: "When ye sin so against the brethren, and wound their weak conscience, ye sin against Christ. Wherefore, if meat maketh my brother to offend, I will eat no flesh while the world standeth, lest I make my brother to offend" (KJV).

Today I am still glad I didn't drink the wine myself, but I wish I hadn't made that poor old 400-pound hog drunk. I do value my influence more, however, than the enjoyment of the taste of a glass of wine.

Confronting Ciriticism

My father was killed in the coal mines when I was three. Being a half-orphan, people were sorry for me. Therefore, they were kind to me.

I grew up in the country where everyone was respectable toward each other. Saying unkind things about others was completely out of my vocabulary. Then being married to a preacher for thirty-two years, I was always respected. Later when I entered the business world, I was totally unprepared to combat what we call professional jealousy.

I had been a director for a few short months and things were really booming. This was the time our company was giving golden goblets for a $1,000 order. I was training goblet winners. We were having fantastic sales meetings every Monday, so I was happy with my unit. My national sales director was proud of me too.

At the same time there was a director in my town who was failing. All of a sudden, boom! Things began to fall apart. My world started tumbling. When I would deliver products, people would tell me things that this director had said about me. All of a sudden, my sales meetings started to drop off. My goblet winners started quitting. I saw my unit going down the drain. I started investigating. The director who was failing had secured the help of her director to really destroy me by telling my girls I didn't train right and the company was dissatisfied with me, that I was buying my new recruits orders to get them. I heard some terrible things being said which were totally untrue. I started getting letters from the officers as to some things I was doing that I should not. I lost eight goblet winners.

Poor me! I cried, staying awake at night. I prayed, read the 91st Psalm, and walked the floor. I was so unprepared for this sort of criticism.

My national sales director, Susie Vickers, called me and said "Don't let this get you down." I had not even made production that month.

Then the answer came—from within myself. I told myself I would just recruit more people. This I did. I told myself I was going to refuse to allow myself to be destroyed.

The next year I was Queen of Recruiting. My unit sold $250,000 worth of product. I truly believe we can be hurt by someone only if we will allow ourselves to be hurt. If I hear something anyone says about me that is not true, I don't give it any attention whatsoever.

I remember what a friend told me one time when I congratulated him for a promotion: "Mary, the higher up on the ladder of life you climb, the better view people will have of you to cast rocks at you." I now remember those words and when I hear something uncomplimentary, I feel I am just a little higher up on the ladder of life. And believe me, I am going to keep climbing until Jesus comes to get me, because I love it high!

CHAPTER III

A CORPORATE TESTIMONY

The Mary Kay Company is the greatest company in the whole world. You may search the whole world over and you would never find a company that cares and does as much for the employees as Mary Kay Company does for us.

I do not know of any other company that remembers every employee with a gift. On each anniversary there is a gift. The Mary Kay Company really cares about its employees.

To my knowledge the Mary Kay Company is the only company that has as its philosophy, God first, family second, career third. Most companies demand first consideration to themselves.

We who have been with the company look forward with much enthusiasm and expectation to seeing Mary Kay and her staff when we attend the meetings in Dallas. We must follow company policies. When we sign our beauty case agreement, we agree to abide by the policy of the company. I certainly advise everyone to avoid short cuts and always follow these policies. Mary Kay has set up the policies and it is a must that we never try another way; when we do we will get into trouble.

For instance, there was a lady in a town about 100 miles from me who wrote asking for information about coming into the company. At this time I was overly anxious to find recruits any place I could find them.

After loading my care with products, I took off for this town to find my consultant-to-be. I located her and she wanted to come into the company. I knew at once this woman was not the type of consultant we needed. However, her husband was very anxious for her to get into the company and I was so eager to get a consultant. So, against my better judgment, we filled out the beauty case agreement.

Being Saturday evening, I wanted to get back in town Sunday morning. They gave me a check for the case and her first order. I spent the night with them and left Sunday morning with the check. These people had a business and I felt there was no danger of their check bouncing. Monday morning I rushed down and deposited their check in my account and gave my personal check for their order. I felt real proud of a new recruit.

About one week later, the check returned. I called the lady and told her what happened. She promised to mail me the money the next day. One week went by, another week, no money. By this time I began to fear I would not get my money. So I told her she must pick up this check or I would have to turn it in. You can readily see that I got off to a bad start with my new consultant. This was the only order she ever made.

I thought this had taught me a lesson that I would never forget. But a year later, I had another case where I let my eagerness let a consultant get the better of me. I didn't follow company policy as I should have. A girl came to my home and wanted to recruit. I quickly helped her fill out her beauty case agreement. After we had it filled out, she said, "I won't have the money until Friday, but Friday I can have the money for my case and the order too." This was on a Tuesday. In my eagerness to get a consultant, I suggested that I send in the money for the case and the order and get her money Friday. She was employed with a local department store and said her payday was Friday. So I literally ran to the bank and got the cashier's check with my personal check. Friday I ran down to pick up my money and she was not home. For days I hunted for my new consultant. When I found her, she quickly announced that she had changed her mind and was not going to sell Mary Kay.

Luckily for me I had requested the company to send the order to me. So in my distress I started trying to find another consultant to take the beauty case. One month went by. On Monday morning at the sales meeting this girl showed up as a new recruit for another consultant. I quickly explained that the girl was on the Mary Kay IBM as a consultant and could not be recruited by another.

The consultant who tried to recruit her started the rumor that I was ordering orders for my recruits. I had a terrible time living through this sally because I failed to follow company policy.

Our company pays us a fantastic commission and bonuses. If we want a raise, all we have to do is hold another show. I don't know of a company any place where employees can make as big a salary as she wants to and work the hours she wants to. We set our own income. If we don't do well we have no one to blame but ourselves. We have the product and the people need it. They have the money to buy it. If we don't know how to sell it, it is solely our own fault.

We are furnished by the company all the tools we need to sell the product: Mary Kay's manual with twenty years' experience laid out in a tape, our flip chart, plus our director's training at training classes, and sales meetings.

Really, there is no ceiling on what you can do. It's up to you!!

I believe God had a purpose for me when I joined Mary Kay Company. On my way to church one morning I looked across the way into West County Park here in Odessa. I saw the beautiful trees with their limbs all spread out and covered with beautiful rich green leaves. I thought, "How beautiful the trees are." I remembered twenty-five years ago those same trees were only small saplings. My mind went back over the years thinking of all the care that had gone into producing these trees, the feeding and watering. My mind then drifted to why these trees were placed in this park. In this place twenty-five years ago, the park was barren, the sun shone hot on the ground, and Ector County park officials wanted to plant some trees with shade so people could sit under the trees and enjoy themselves. I thought, "My, how they have grown." I then thought how I, too, have grown in the twenty-five years, just like the trees. God placed me here and I believed He had a purpose. Just as the employees watered and fed the trees, God has fed me with His Holy Spirit, His Word.

Today those trees are a blessing to many people and I want to think I have been a blessing to many lives. I am quite sure that through the years the storms have broken the limbs, the wind has blown the leaves away, but the trees just bided their time and grew some more. I, too, have been through the storms and my heart has been broken several times. Sometimes I felt I would never be of any value to anyone, but I, like the trees, have from time to time taken new life and gone on. These trees will stand many more years and continue to be a blessing to many more people. I sincerely hope I can be a greater blessing to mankind. The more I looked at the trees, I thought of the storms, wind, rain, and sunshine they had withstood; and still they stood tall and beautiful because they were there for a purpose.

In spite of many disappointments in these past years, by the grace of God, I will stand.

When the records are exposed, we will know just how much we have helped other people. I know many people have blessed my life and they have helped me grow just as the trees in the park have grown.

Let your mind drift for a minute to all the wonderful people you have met who are consultants, directors, and national directors. I believe we have the finest people in our company that can be found in this world.

Like the trees in the park, they stand out in the crowd, offering their knowledge and energy to help every one around. As a Mary Kay consultant, you can sit in the shade of their knowledge and take advantage of the opportunity to soak up wisdom.

CHAPTER IV

SUCCESS THROUGH ORGANIZATION

I realized at the very start I had to get organized.

My first step was to organize my product. After searching around for cabinets that could be locked, I had shelves built into one of my closets and changed all my books from my book case. I bought a beauty shop case for fifty dollars and started organizing my product.

My next step was to get containers to put different things in. I went to the variety store and bought plastic silverware trays to keep my Day Radiances in. I used plastic boxes for mascara bath; black and white plastic trays for pencils—all colors. I used one shelf in the metal cabinet for colognes and another cabinet for Mr. K, using each shelf for different things. Then I had extra shelves for shampoos, hair spray, and conditioner. In other words, my Mary Kay room looks like a drug store.

Also, I found a beauty shop going out of business and bought the wall section for its mirrors. My next step was to put a large dining table and chairs in my Mary Kay room.

Now that my Mary Kay room was organized, I knew I needed to organize my house. This was a major operation! I had saved all of my panty hose and other undergarments for years and I had pajamas and gowns that had not been used in ten years. Also, I had dresses hanging in my closets that would never be worn by me. My kitchen cabinets were crammed full. Each drawer had to be pushed and pushed before it would close.

I started pulling out those panties that I never intended to use, those hose that had runs in them. Since I sew, I had boxes of quilt pieces. So I began boxing pieces of materials and boxing kitchen utensils—that egg beater that I had saved for years, those old dishes, glasses, frying pans and coffee pots. In fact, I boxed just about everything you could mention. They could all be sent to needy people and the result was that my house was organized. Now I must organize myself.

Organize Inwardly

Before you can organize outwardly by the priority system, you must first determine inwardly that you will *not* give mental recognition to defeat and that you will think only in terms of VICTORY AND SUCCESS! Consider the following questions each day and check your attitude.

—Do my goals reflect a dynamic inward desire for success in a Mary Kay Career?

—Are my plans concretely set and framed in my mind as well as drafted by pen and paper?

—Is my emotional system supercharged and constantly emitting Go—Go, Win—Win, Charge—Charge, and similar signals proving my desire to succeed?

—Do I feel at the start of each day an urgency to be of service to others, in making them prettier, and sharing a Mary Kay career?

—Do I possess *confidence*, that calm assurance which speaks to the world that I am programmed for success and nothing can defeat me?

—Do I possess the *absolute determination* to accomplish my goals, and can I see beyond the clouds, obstacles, and circumstances to the wonderful world of my personal success?

Organize by the Priority System

Mary Kay tells us that consultants wear many hats—wife, mother, housekeeper, chauffeur, and Mary Kay consultant—all important! The only way all this can be accomplished is to organize by the priority system—or *first* things *first*. Sort out the daily tasks that must be done—but not necessarily by you. For instance, it is ridiculous for you to be home ironing, washing, or cleaning floors at $1 an hour. Have a maid to do this for you and hold one or two shows on the "maid's day." If you have someone do these things while you are out, you will not have to neglect your family or husband when you are at home. You still will have more time for yourself and your family.

Now that you've removed these time-consuming tasks from your schedule, plan every day as though you worked in an office. Get some copies of a Weekly Plan Sheet (order under sales aids) and work out your full week. Your week's plan (priority system) should include two sections, both vitally essential to your overall achievement and success:

1. Your Daily Business Activities:
   a. Have at least two shows a day. Give the best booking talks and recruiting talks. This will assure you of future hostesses, prospective recruits, and good sales.
   b. Use the telephone every day for thirty minutes to an hour: Choose the best time (preferably in

the morning from eight to nine) to call pink tickets, for booking additional shows or making appointments with prospective recruits. Try to do this at a regular time each day. When calling pink tickets, always ask for referrals; ask if they know anyone who would like to do what you are doing. Don't forget to offer her the opportunity. You must have a constant supply of future hostesses and prospective recruits to ensure success in this business.

c. Set aside a time for self-improvement. Read the manual regularly, read motivation books, and read beauty magazines on helpful hints for skin care and makeup. Daily Bible reading should be a must.

d. Visualize with a daily meditation period. Turn off the "motor" and relax, letting your mind visualize the completion of your goals and dreams. Build some new air castles. This is the time you visualize yourself as a super consultant, as a Top Director, or Top Recruiter. Have pen and paper handy to record new ideas that come to mind as you float through the private world of your successful future.

e. Each evening plan for a dynamic tomorrow. A few minutes spent in planning tomorrow's activity via the priority system will create sunny skies for you while there are storm clouds for everyone else. (Use "Six Most Important Things List.") If you don't get everything done, you have at least given priority to the most important things.

f. Review your short range and long range goals. Each day review your goals. Discuss them with your family and friends and let the whole world know you plan to be a success.

2. Your Daily Social and Family Activities:
   Each day in a planned environment there is time
   for fun, hobbies, family, and benevolent activities.
   There is no way to plan these activities as to their
   importance since each family will feel differently
   about what they wish to do. A general guideline
   would include the following activities:
   1. Recreation
   2. Hobbies
   3. Family fun
   4. Church activities
   5. Benevolent work

CHAPTER V

McDOWELL DIRECTIONS

Helpful Harrys

Don't let anyone detour you from your goal as you ascend to the top of your career.

You will attract many different companies that will want you to take on their product as a sideline. Don't do it. I have found that no one can chase two rabbits at the same time. If they do, their pace will be slowed and they will not catch either one!

I have had many, many different people contact me; and believe me, some of their salesmen are so sharp, they can talk you into anything if you don't keep your head. They will paint such attractive pictures that you will be persuaded if you are not careful.

I had one company send a special person clear across these United States and he spent one whole week here in my town trying to pressure me into his company. And he came so near it was frightening. I always stayed within my dream and you should too.

No company can give you what Mary Kay does. And it is a full time business and it will give you all the money you need if you will make it so. It's up to you. You are in the driver's seat.

I did not fully understand what Mary Kay was saying when she would say, "There is no ceiling on your income" until I was in the company many years. I certainly know now.

I spoke to a school one week on Career Day. And how happy I was to take Helen McVoy's photocopied check for $40,000 for one month's earnings and display it to those students.

You have the same opportunity that Helen has. You will begin with the same case. Who knows? Someone reading this book may break her record someday. Why not let that someone be you? You can, you know.

Another warning. Don't buy all the things that come in the mail recommended to help you in your business. All the mail brought to my door has from three to four different things suggested to help me in my business. I received two farm machinery catalogues this week along with a letter attached telling me how much the machines would help me in my business. Sound ridiculous? Most of the offers sound just about as bad. So many companies tell you how to run your business . . . you stay with Mary Kay's plan and it will keep you on the right path.

Another warning concerns advertising companies. One advertising company called me one day, read off the story about my being crowned in Dallas as Queen, and asked if that were correct. I replied, "Yes." He then asked if he had my permission to run it in his paper in a nearby city. I got all excited and thought, "Gee, that would be nice." I had wanted to get some recruits in that town. So I said yes. But I wanted to read it before he ran it and also after he ran it. I waited and waited to see him and read what he had written about me. Two months went by. One day I received a bill for $109 for the story which he called an advertisement. I wrote a note and returned the bill refusing to pay it. In a few days, I received a phone call informing me I owed $109 for advertising in such and such a paper. I told the lady how the man approached me, how the conversation ran, and that I had not seen the paper to see what did run in it. She told me she would mail me one. (Remember this was nearly three months after the story should have run.) I said, "No, I don't want to see the paper because I refuse to pay."

Another two months went by and I received a letter from their attorney threatening to sue me if I did not pay it in ten days. I turned it over to the Better Business Bureau. That was the last of that matter.

So be on the lookout for frauds. When I first started in my career, I was very enthusiastic and wanted to grab every gimmick. Later I learned through experience that this is not wise. Stay with the manual. It is *Gold*.

Doubts and Discouragement

There are so many ways discouragement can come to you and it can come from many directions.

Discouragement comes from no bookings. You say, "I called ten people and only one booked." Don't let this throw you. If you get one out of ten, this is the national average. If you have trouble booking, tell yourself you are just going to learn more about booking.

I have become discouraged many times because I was not booking as well as I thought I ought to. One thing I would do when these times came was to get in the car and drive around and look at the many, many houses in my town. And then I would tell myself: There are a lot of people out there and they are all buying some type of cosmetic and I have the best; so I will just get busy and tell them about mine.

Another thing I would do was to buy something I had to pay for in a limited time. This would help me forget my discouragements and my mind would start spinning, thinking of different things to do.

Plus I make it a practice to ask every person I come in contact with. One example—the plumber when he comes. I ask him if his wife uses Mary Kay. If he said no I would quickly ask, "Would you mind if I called her and told her you said to call her and arrange a facial?" Once I got the facial I turned it into a show. I did this with every person who came to my home to do any type of work. I even booked the meter reader. These tricks will get you going again.

I have known some girls to say their husbands did not approve of their selling. If this is your case, just maybe he is just wanting you to prove to him you can do it! I had one real good consultant who is good at selling and whose husband was delighted when she came into Mary Kay. However, he told her he was buying only one order for her and she would have to manage her money so she could order next time—that he would not finance her again.

She sold $500 her first week. The next week she called me and said, "Mary, what am I going to do? I have two shows booked and another to sell." I asked her if she saved her money to order with. She said, "No, I bought school clothes with the money for my kids." And now her husband would not let her have any more to order. I told her, "Now, Maria, I am going to arrange for you to borrow this order on your own, but you must promise me that you won't spend it this time." She vowed she would not. I went to the bank and she borrowed $500 more for an order. I asked the loan officer before we arrived by phone to instruct her not to spend her money so she could order. This he did. I felt good thinking she would follow through. I kept explaining, "Now, Maria, you are a business woman and you must learn to handle your money properly." A few days later she called me again and said "Mary, I have no product to sell and have shows booked and my husband won't let me borrow again."

I lost a good consultant simply because she didn't handle her business like a business. This is a big business and we must handle it like professionals.

Some consultants have told me their husbands didn't want them to be gone when he was home. If this is the problem you have, just arrange to have your shows when he is at work. Don't give up and quit. Just get yourself organized so you can be with him when he is home.

One of the things I found that discouraged me when I first started my career was that I would use my money for things I felt I really needed and would not be prepared to order when I needed products.

I learned to solve this problem before too long. When I caught myself in this position, I gave some serious thought to the problem. Solution: Borrow from the bank enough to start all over again and open a separate account and refuse to use this money for anything else.

I would tell myself, "Now, Mary, you would have to do without the money if you were not selling Mary Kay. And since you are, you must by all means protect your career."

Being on my own before my stock was built up, if my house payment was due, I would take the house payment and place my order and then get out and sell enough the next two days for my house payment.

Another discouragement for so many is that the shows don't always hold. There again, don't let this discourage you. Solve this problem by having eight shows per week, so if three cancel, you will still have five. There again, be sure you have coached your hostess well and that you have studied your chapter on avoiding cancellations. Always remember there is an answer to every problem. If you come to a mountain, just figure some way to climb over it or go around it. There will be a way. I promise you.

Sometimes God allows us to have problems so when we solve them, we are much stronger. Remember any old fish can swim downstream, but it takes a good one to swim upstream.

Determine within yourself that come what may, you are going to stay with this wonderful opportunity. You're going to go to the top. And no one, but no one, is going to stop you! And by all means, stay away from negative people. In fact, run from them. They are in every family . . . someone who is ready to say you can't do it.

I have had girls tell me their husbands told them they had not made anything in Mary Kay. To which I always reply, "You have to make money when you make two dollars for one. How can anyone be senseless enough to say you didn't make any money when I know that when you double your money, you have made money."

I have experienced most of all these different things that I have been writing about. But never did I ever give up. And you must not either because there is a big pink world out there and all you have to do to own your share of it is to sell.

You have the people. They have the money, and you have the product. The very best product!

Harness Hatred

One of the most important things I have learned in my Mary Kay career is that we, positively, must not allow jealousy, hatred, or malice to remain in our hearts. We must take it out even if it hurts like a surgeon using a knife. Take it out.

Being a pampered orphan that everyone was sorry for, I developed a feeling that everyone should be nice and kind, and the word jealousy was foreign to me. When I married, I married a preacher, and people respected me as a preacher's wife. When I entered the business world I had a great awakening. I had to deal with people who were jealous and unkind. Let's face it. Everyone is not going to like us. If we stood on our head to please them, they will not like us any better. So you must learn early to face rejection and go on. You must act as if nothing happened and just learn to not let things hurt you.

I had a friend one time tell me that when someone said ugly things about me to picture myself as an elephant going down the street with red ants digging and nibbling at my toes.

We must not let hatred enter our hearts. We must not allow it to stay. Remember someone needs to be big and it might as well be you.

I have a beautiful story to tell you that illustrates what I am trying to say.

I happened in Bristol, Virginia in 1932. The town was proud of its two iron works plants, two overall factories, two dress manufacturers, an airplane plant, a coffin assembly plant, and, of course, a reasonable number of retail merchants.

I lived and worked in Bristol and, like most others, just took things for granted. Then one day, without warning, tragedy struck. All the lights went out. That night the town was engulfed in complete darkness. The ominous silence was frightening. The whole town was at a standstill.

Men worked feverishly trying to solve the mystery and correct the problem. Two days and nights stretched into three and still no solution. Townspeople were getting panicky. All factories were shut down; people were out of work; many couldn't believe what was happening. Others prayed. Was this the work of the devil or was God trying to tell us something?

Then, almost as suddenly as the blackout occurred, the problem was solved. The lights were back on. The town seemed to breathe a sigh of relief. In a short time, all was back to normal.

A small boy playing around in the building that supplied the electricity for the town had slipped a cigarette paper somewhere in the dynamo causing a short circuit. They said later that it was like finding a needle in a haystack.

As I listened to people talking about this happening, I began thinking about our own lives. When we allow petty jealousy, hatred, unforgiveness, selfishness, and greed to dominate our thinking, we can short-circuit ourselves from God, leaving us in darkness. (Read I Peter 2:12.) I could be like the cigarette paper, something small blocking the Holy Spirit and keeping our blessings from us.

We may not realize that we are separating ourselves from God because we have failed to take the time to analyze ourselves or have failed to admit we have sin. We are inclined to justify ourselves. Just as the lights went out when the power failed, joy and love will go out of our lives when we lose touch with God.

Hate will destroy our integrity. The Bible teaches us not to hate and not to covet. When we go against anything the Bible teaches, it will hurt us. We must let it go. If we don't give it up because we are powerless to do so, let us ask God to remove it. There is strong medical evidence that hate even causes bodily diseases.

Up in the hills of Tennessee where I once lived, we had a saying that illustrates my point. "You can't keep birds from flying over your head, but you can keep them from building nests in your hair." The devil wants us to hate, to harbor envy and jealousy. Don't let him conquer and thus turn out the lights in your heart.

Give for Success

If you want to be successful in your Mary Kay career, give of your income to God's causes. I believe in tithing. That's what I practice and have for many years. We must make a decision as to how we are going to share our income. We don't want to earn money for money alone; we need to share. You must decide for yourself.

Life is made up of decisions and every good thing happens because we have made the right decision. Every bad thing happens because we made the wrong decision.

The greatest decision I ever made in my whole life was made standing on a street corner in Bristol, Virginia, in 1932. We were in the midst of the deep depression. My husband's job had completely stopped. We were living in Middlesboro, Kentucky at the time. No jobs of any kind were to be found. Our food ran out. We were renting a small house for $12 a month. Our utility bills had to be paid, but we had no job, no funds.

My husband called me into the living room for a conference and told me the doctors had explained to him that his nervous system had completely broken under the strain and the doctors had ordered him to enter the government hospital in Johnson City, Tennessee, for treatment. Since he was a World War I veteran, this treatment would be free. He explained to me that he might be there a couple of years before he recovered. He said that I should sell our furniture for whatever I could get out of it and go home to my mother. My mother's husband had been in bed at this time two years with a stroke. They lived on a large farm and Mother had to spend all her time with him. Leonard, my husband, felt I could be of help to her, and of course there was plenty of food there. At least we would be comfortable until he got well.

These were my exact words in reply: "No, when I married you, I married you to spend my life with you and not run home to Mother. I will make it somehow." Bless his darling heart, he said, "How on earth can you make it?" I said, "Somehow." Little did I know how hard the way would be. However, I accepted it and started planning.

I had an aunt who lived in Bristol, Virginia, which was only about 25 miles from where my husband would be in the hospital. How would I get to Bristol? God made a way. My aunt's friend in Middlesboro was going to Bristol in a few days in a truck and he agreed to take me and my son and my few belongings along for $5.00. I gladly accepted the offer. The government paid the fare for my husband to the hospital.

Now followed the task of getting my furniture sold. I found a buyer who paid me fifteen dollars for my whole houseful of furniture, except one bed, one chair, one dresser, and a trunk that I took along. I had twelve dollars in money that I earned for working two weeks as a waitress before I left. Off we went to Virginia to find a new life—and what a new life it was.

One of the customers, Mr. Wall, at the restaurant where I worked told me should I need references for work when I arrived in Bristol, to use his name. He owned an overall factory there. When we arrived, I rented one of my aunt's rooms for five dollars per month and paid my share of the utilities. I bought an oil stove to cook on, got all set up, and started to look for work. People were standing in lines to merely get a loaf of bread. Incidentially, bread sold for five cents a loaf, eggs for five cents per dozen. Any place that hired people would have 75 to 100 people standing all day hoping to get a job. I walked for two weeks trying to find work—housework, waitress work, just anything. In the meantime, my twelve dollars was slowly slipping away. I became desperate. I was so afraid of the future, not only for myself, but for my darling son. I was afraid we would not have food.

I had never really applied in the right way for a job. In fact, I didn't know how. In great desperation I found courage to go to the overall factory to see if I could get a job. All the way to the factory, I could hear those machines roaring, making so much noise. In Middlesboro I had passed the overall factory there every day and would always say, "I could never work in there because of all the noise those machines make." Now here I was ready to fall on my knees and beg for a job in one.

When I entered the room where all the people were waiting, hoping to get hired, I pushed my way through, edged up to the counter and asked the girl behind it if I could speak to Mr. Holt. Mr. Holt was the superintendent of the factory. She went out and got him and when he came out, he looked quite astonished that I would be so brazen. I said, "Mr. Holt, I need a job. I have just come to town and Mr. Wall told me if I needed a reference, he would gladly give me one. Do you have anything I can do?" He said, "I don't today but come back tomorrow."

Seven o'clock the next morning I was there standing in the same big crowd hoping to get a job. No one was hired that day. He said, "Come back tomorrow." I did this for two straight weeks. Now my money was just about gone.

On the twelfth day, Mr. Holt came out and picked me

out of the crowd and took me upstairs and ordered the forewoman to start me sewing pockets on overalls. I had to sew on fifty pockets for ten cents. How glad I was to get the job! My first two weeks I made $4.27. This furnished us food. My rent was not due yet. The next two weeks I made the same amount. Now I was getting very, very worried. I was so afraid. At this time I was a Christian but had never learned to turn my problems all over to God. I felt I had to do it myself. We would go to the factory and sit all day and maybe get two or three ten-cent bundles the whole day. When a bundle came through to be sewed, we would grab it like a hungry dog grabbing a bone.

One day we had spent the whole day sitting hoping to get a bundle of pockets to sew on. But no work. Late that afternoon Mr. Holt came out and told us to go home and he would have someone call us when they had work.

Walking home that afternoon, I had such a heavy heart. What on earth could I do? No one loaned money in those days. No one extended credit. So what was I to do? I was stumbling along, my eyes so full of tears I could hardly walk. I stopped for a crossing at Fairmont and Commonwealth Avenues. While I was waiting at the crossing, the words of David came to me as clearly as if someone were standing by my side. "I once was young and now I am old and I have never seen the righteous forsaken or his seed begging bread." I stood very still because I knew these promises were to me. I knew that I belonged to God because He had given His Son Who saved me when I was only fourteen years old. At this time, I was twenty-eight. Right there that day I made the decision to take Jesus as my partner in all my affairs.

I said, "Dear God, if you will give me work so I can provide for my child, I will give you at least a tenth of everything that comes into my hand." My tears were all gone. My fear was all gone, and I had complete confidence that I had my hand in the Master's hand. Never again would I worry that I would starve. The words of Malachi 3:8-10 came to be my constant companion.

I have lived with those words ringing in my ears all these years. This was the greatest decision I ever made. From that day to this, I have never been afraid anymore. I have always had a complete assurance that come what may, I had my hand in the Master's and it would come out all right.

He has poured out His blessing on me in such a marvelous way. He has given me not only all I needed, but He has given me everything in a financial way I could ever want. I praise His name that I made the right decision that day.

Invest in Activities

Become active in your community. But don't let yourself become loaded down.

I belonged to most every club in town before I came into Mary Kay. The lady who recruited me knew this; that is why she sought me out to find someone to sell. You need all the exposure you can get, so get into organizations; but don't let them load you down with offices and duties. I spent a lot of time in organizations before I entered into my career. In fact, I spent more money on dinners, luncheons, and breakfasts than I did on all my living expenses.

Today I belong and attend but refuse to let people use too much of my time. Do, by all means, join the Chamber of Commerce in your town. Of course your dues are deductible. And this will bring you into focus with the Better Business Bureau people.

Also register with the Better Business Bureau. I hold the elections in my precinct and have been precinct chairman for years. This only takes about four days out of my year and has proven to be profitable in that I meet and learn the voters in my area.

I also have served nine years on the park board. This threw me directly into contact with wide coverage of people. At the present time, I am chairman of the Children's Services Board and have served on this board for many years. I also belong to the City Service and Democratic Women's Club. These provide me with a wide range of people to work with and has proven very valuable to me. In other words, my town knows that I am a Mary Kay Director.

All of this does carry a great deal of responsibility. I have to be very straight in all my dealings because I know I have to project the Mary Kay image in everything—not just part. But I love the role I play and it makes me feel important. My dearest friends are the mayor, county judge, and all the elected city officials and county officers.

For Valentines Day last year I wrapped Mr. Kalotions in net and ribbon and carried every policeman a Valentine gift.

Try to make friends with everyone. Make friends with your Water Department employees of your city. Ask them to let you come in and obtain a list of the newcomers which they obtain from new hookups. This will give you more people to contact than you can imagine.

When you call them, tell them that you have a gift for them to welcome them to town and have some small bath gel lotion and Mr. K-nines wrapped in net and ribbon and give them one. Ask them to come to your home. Call enough that you will have six to hold a show at one time.

It takes years of building your business before they will seek you out to buy.

You definitely cannot just order your product, put it on the shelf, and expect to build a good business. You must get out of the house and make yourself known. Get involved!

Goal Setting

I learned early to set goals. Here is a simple illustration:

Draw yourself a square on a poster board—a twelve-inch square. In this square, don't have anything. Just empty space. This illustrates how it is when you don't have a goal.

Now put circles around and around. This represents when you come into Mary Kay with a lot of enthusiasm but not goals. Now draw a large $500 in the center and say, "This is my goal for the month." Now you have set a goal. The next step is to make plans how you are going to reach your goal.

Make yourself a chart for the month. Divide it into weeks. You now know you have to have $125 per week. Divide the week into five days. Now you know how much you need to see each day. Sixteen dollars and seventy-five cents per day will do it or $125 a show each week will do it.

Get yourself a small blackboard. Write across the top of the board Monday-Tuesday-Wednesday-Thursday-Friday-Saturday. Monday morning, get out of bed telling yourself you have to sell $25 today. Everytime you sell something, even if only an eye-pencil, jot it down on the board. Before you go to bed at night, add up what you have sold that day. Start every day doing the same thing and watch your sales grow.

Someone has said that when you set your goals, the

universe will work for you. I don't know what makes it work. But it will, I promise you. Consistency is the key to success. This is the way I did it. Every week I would set my goals higher. Monthly, weekly and by the day. I now sell $150 per day easily.

Now for your long-range goals.

If you want to be on stage at seminar for sales, you know what you have to do. You have to have $14,000 wholesale for the year. So you know you are going to have to sell $1,660 per month. Divide it in months, weeks, and day.

Now don't say you can't do it. I know you can. I have been on stage for sales six times as of this writing.

All right, set your goal to become a Director. You know this is where you ought to be. You know you really need fourteen consultants to become a Director. The company says twelve, but I think you will be more effective if you have fourteen.

You can easily make Director in six months. Two consultants a month will do it. Why not set your goal for a recruit each week? I know you can do this, too.

The secret is to have a show each day. Share your Mary Kay experience with at least one girl at each show. Think about this: If you have a show each day and you have an average of three people at each show, this gives you about fifteen people from whom you can select one each week.

See how easy it is!

Setting a goal is only the beginning. Also keep in mind that procrastination is like cobwebs. They can start with a little procrastination here and a little there and before you know it, they are like cables. They will rob you of your success. A good thing is to remember what some great wise man said many years ago: Do not put off until tomorrow the things you should be doing today. *And once a task you have begun, never leave it until it's done!*

When I first started my Mary Kay career, I disciplined myself to reach my goals. I would set a goal and get all enthusiastic before I went to bed, promising myself I would work hard tomorrow. I would get up fully intending to put in a full day's work because I had a goal to reach. Then the phone would ring, a friend had called to visit. By the time I got through with her, a neighbor would come by for coffee. By the time she left and we had drunk coffee I would remember that I had to mop the kitchen, etc.

You have to rearrange your life and get that discipline to working. Goal setting is a place to start.

Specific Examples of Goal Setting

I knew if I was to be the person I wanted to be, I had to do enough to reflect that person I wanted to be. So I had to decide what I would do.

My first job was to sell $1,000 per month (fifty dollars each day chart). My first month, my sales were $1,000. My prize from Mary Kay was a gold goblet and a Polaroid camera, and an opportunity to attend the gold goblet banquet. This was the most wonderful moment of my life. My first Mary Kay banquet! My dress for the occasion was beautiful. Our seminar was held at the Marriott Hotel in Dallas. The meeting room was decorated more beautifully than Hollywood's Oscar award meeting place. There was a beautiful archway arranged. Mary Kay stood on one side and presented the gold goblet as we came in. Erma Thompson stood on the other side and presented us a beautiful orchid. A young escort stood ready to escort us down the red carpet aisle. The crowd stood and cheered as we walked down the aisle. To me this was one of the greatest moments of my life.

This inflated my ego. I loved the recognition.

Now in my mind I realized I had to set goals. At all the meetings we attended, they talked about goal setting. Goals were the most popular subject. I wanted to set goals, but no one explained how to reach them.

I learned I was only wishing. Then I learned step by step how to reach goals. So I want to explain how to reach your goals.

Decide how much money you want to earn. Or how much recognition do you want. Do you want to be Director? If you do, hold one or two shows each day for five days. Keep Saturday and Sunday free.

One show each day will run like this—if you know your product well and learn to hold good shows. You must coach your hostess well. Let's say she has six guests:

To sell five out of six—work nets $315 and a profit of $157.50. Two hours work.

Five shows—ten hours: work nets $1,575 and a profit of $787.

Twenty shows—forty hours: work nets $6,300 and a profit of $3,150.

If you have five people at each show, this will give you 100 people to get your recruits from. You should have at least five recruits from 100 people. Remember this is only ten hours each week. Easy? Sure it is. The thing to do is plan for what you want.

If you want to be Queen of Sales, for instance, you can hold twenty shows each month. You will have to order at least $300 each month. This will give you enough sales that you can be Queen of Sales.

To become Queen, I set my goal to sell $2,500 each month and ordered $2,500 wholesale each month. If I missed one month, I picked it up the next for the 12 months. At the end of that time I had $27,900. This made me Queen. So you see how I came to reach my goal.

Let's say you want to be Queen of Recruiting. Twenty-four qualified recruits will put you in Queen's Court. So I set my goal for three each month and come seminar time, I had forth-two which made me queen.

To get my recruits each month I take a poster board, cut out five beautiful girls' pictures and then I start searching for the girls who resemble my pin-up girls. When I get one, her name is taped to the pictures. Then my search is on for the next and the next. I have had fourteen gold medals and got them all in this manner.

Let me tell you about my beautiful black girl. One particular month I put up my poster, and instead of five pictures, I put up six. One was a black girl. My remarks to my secretary was, "This month I want a pretty black girl." I found a picture in a magazine of a beautiful black girl. That month I was extremely busy and didn't really try to find my black girl. So the next month, her picture went up first. I made no effort whatsoever to reach her. But the first week of the month, the doorbell rang and when I opened the door, there stood my beautiful black girl. She was so much like the picture I could hardly go into my interview.

When I told her Mary Kay's philosophy is God first, your family second, and your career third, she broke into a beautiful smile and said, "This is for me because I have a group of young people at my church I am working with, and I have to work to go to college." Tears streamed down my face and I said, "Annette, God sent you here today. Look up there at your picture." And I believe with my whole heart that He did.

I have never yet set a goal and really worked toward it

without reaching it. My earnings from Mary Kay Cosmetics has helped me reach so many personal goals. When Mary Kay says there is no ceiling on our earnings, it is really true. Where could an older lady make this kind of money other than Mary Kay?

This is a letter that I send out to my consultants:

Dear Consultant:

I have just found something that excites me tremendously. Take your pencil right now and put this plan down and start working it and I will see you on stage next seminar.

Get out of bed each morning, dress yourself, get your face made, be ready to go to work by nine o'clock. Book a show for each day of the week. Let's say, five shows. Leave Saturday and Sunday open for yourself and for the Lord. Hold one show each day. Just think. Two hours each day for your show, ten hours per week, six people at each show. Let's say you sell five people. This will give you $152.50 each day. Now for the week you would have $762.50 for ten hours work. Now let's say you do this for four weeks. You would have $3,500 for the month and a profit of $2,695 and all for only 40 hours for four weeks.

Now don't say you can't do it. I know you can because I have done this once and over. You have to learn to book. You have to learn to sell. Your manual will tell you word for word how to do it. Not only will you be on stage for sales, you can be on stage for recruiting. At each show you will have six people to select a recruit from. You will have twenty-four people in the month from which to select recruits. Study your recruiting in your manual plus all the materials I send you.

Another thing you can do is hire someone to help you with your housework, babysitting, etc., and deduct from your income tax.

Come on now and let's go to the top this year. I know you can do it. I will be listening to hear from you.

Love,
Mary

Keep Happy

I am anxious for you to be a happy person as you reach toward your goals in life.

I think I have found a secret of how to be happy. Each morning when you arise for the day, think of something you can do for others. Remembering all you put into the lives of others will come back into your own.

My Mary Kay career has opened the doors to many lives I have been able to touch. Your consultants and customers have problems and you can pray with them and counsel with them.

I had the joy of leading a consultant to a new life in Christ in my living room recently. She was so burdened down with worry and cares that she could not work. But she arose from her knees happy. Her burden had been lifted. This is true happiness.

We should be constantly ready to look around us and help those we can help. I don't mean give money. I mean give of ourselves. Sometimes I think we are more ready to give money than get involved in the lives of others who might need us.

While making a business trip to Bakersfield, California, some time ago, I was forced to change planes in San Francisco. Because of the nature of my trip, I had taken along more than I could handle properly. I had my movie machine that I could not ship, my coat, and much more than I could handle. There were no redcaps near when I got off and it was a long way from one ramp to the next where I had to board. I was about half-way there, struggling along with my things when a young man walked up and said, "Lady, could I help you with your belongings?" "Could you!" I cried. I was so happy to have him offer. Thinking the young man was working to earn some money, I planned to be generous with my tip.

When we arrived at my take-off ramp, I pulled out my purse, thanked him, handing him a large tip. He exclaimed, "Lady, I am here to help people. Should I take your money, I would not receive any blessing from doing it. No, no money, thank you." My heart cried for joy and as I write these words my eyes fill with tears of thanksgiving that there are still young people in this world who want to help people, any place they can find them. I never got the young man's name, but, oh, the prayers I have said for him. And when the book is brought out in heaven, I sincerely believe that young man will receive a reward for helping me while I was in distress.

Won't you pray with me today that my life and your life can be a blessing to many people before we take our flight to our eternal home?

Please give it some thought. Who have you helped today? Jesus said, "As you have done it unto them, you have done it unto me." He also said, "As you did it not unto them, you did it not unto me."

> If you have learned to walk
> a little more sure-footedly than I,
> be patient with my stumbling then
> and know that only as I do my best and try
> may I attain the goal
> for which we both are striving.

If through experience, your soul
has gained heights which I
as yet in dim-lit vision see,
hold out your hand and point the way,
lest from its straightness I should stray,
and walk a mile with me.

    —Author unknown

CHAPTER VI

RULES OF RECRUITING

The Basics

What kind of job would you call an ideal job? Wouldn't it be one that you could work the hours you want to work? A job with shorter hours that gives you more money? A job that would give you prestige while at the same time letting you be your own boss? The Mary Kay opportunity gives you all of these,

Recruiting is just like any other worthwhile endeavor: You must learn how. Once you have mastered recruiting it comes so easy.

1. You must be sold on your company; you can't ask anyone to join anything you don't believe in.
2. You must be in love with your product. You must believe it to be the greatest product produced and marketed today.
3. You must believe in yourself and your abilities to picture Mary Kay and the company in such glowing pictures that your prospect will become excited and want to become a part of the company enough to be willing to do anything reasonable to get the money for her investment.
4. By presenting materials on what others are making, impart to her what she can become once she has launched out her career program. Show her how she can become great too.

I make up recruiting packets (ten or twelve at a time). In these packets I place "Ambitions of American Women," *Reader's Digest* reprint ("It Could Only Happen in America"), a beauty book, a Mr. K instruction sheet, a hair care folder, and a beauty case agreement.

Every person who comes to get a facial is asked many questions about where she works, where she is from, what her husband does, and by the time I am through with her facial, I know quite a bit about her. After I close and get her order, I look straight into her eyes and say, "You really ought to be selling Mary Kay." If she says she works but has been thinking about doing something as a part-time job, I pick up my recruit packet and say, "Take this home with you and read it and call me within two days and let me know what you think of it. "As soon as she is out of the door, I write her name and phone number in my recruit book and jot down the information I got during the facial. If she calls me, I set up an appointment for her and her husband, if she is married. If she does not call me, I call her.

When she comes I show her "The Way of Life" film. Believe me, that film is a must in recruiting. When I finish the film, I take her through my photo album recruiting book. I have the prettiest pictures I can find in the front. I explain how the company was formed and Mary Kay's philosophy about the company. I also show pictures of our distribution centers. My next page is "Mary Kay Presents to You a Golden Opportunity"; the following pages explain the opportunities. I have a map of the U.S.A. and show her that we have the entire U.S.A. as our territories and that no one can squeeze us out. The next page shows that we have shorter hours, that we can be among the Stars. All this is very fulfilling. I show that our company is a reliable one, that we have a superior product, and that we are our own boss.

It is like a self-improvement course in that we sell

beauty; therefore, we want to look pretty. We learn makeup and I explain that there is an art to makeup. We have money to spend and that is beautiful. I explain the tax benefits. While doing this I am qualifying my prospect, unknowing to her. I ask if she owns her home, does she have furniture, does she have one or two cars, etc. By doing this, I know whether she has borrowing power. I have arrangements with a finance company that will loan her money if she owns anything in her name. I explain the difference in a Mary Kay career and a dress show, laundry cleaners, or teaching. I say "You can teach school twenty-five years and when you retire you will probably be making very little more than the day you started. They may present you with a twenty-five dollar watch and serve you with some punch and cookies." I then explain to her that she is going into a wonderful business for herself and she will need something to sell.

If she opened a store she would need goods to sell. Likewise, in Mary Kay she will need products. I tell her the cost of the beauty case and explain its value. I try to get the order with the agreement. I tell her she can start recruiting as soon as she signs the agreement. I then go through the avenue of income and how she can go to the top. I tell them what the top people are making and then I show my prizes and my top check. Then I say, "What do you think?"

If they like it—and they usually do—this is the way I ask my prospective recruits to start their Mary Kay careers. I always ask that they borrow the money, regardless of how much they have in the bank. I tell them if they have savings, borrow it from themselves. If you have it in your checking account, fine. But if you do not have the money, go to the bank and borrow it. If you don't have bank credit, but do have a car, furniture, etc.,

I have arranged with a finance company so you can go to them and borrow against these things.

Now since you are borrowing money, I tell them, you really should borrow $550. But don't let this scare you because I can show you how you can do it. You can borrow $500 for your order and seventy-five dollars for your case. Mary Kay lets us pay the tax when we buy our product, so we don't have to bother with sending in reports on sales tax. We like this very much, but we do have to have it when we order and collect it back as we sell. You should arrange to pay the loan back at fifty dollars a month.

Now open a checking account with your $550 and place your order. Then sell one complete set each month to make your payment. In this manner your budget is not bothered a bit. And you are using another person's money to finance your career. Do you know many people who have gone into business and made a success without using another person's money? "See how easy it is?" I continue to explain.

I tell her I would like for her to have five shows booked by the time she gets her case so she will be ready to place her product at once.

I help them fill out the agreement and go to the bank or finance company and introduce and recommend them for a loan. I stay with her until she opens her checking account, gets her cashier's check, and I take it to the post office before I leave her.

After I had helped two of my consultants fill out their letters of intent recently, my heart filled with so much love and admiration as I looked at these two girls who had in two short months opened up to twenty-five new consultants a new way of life.

I explained to her she has now borrowed her money, so she is now on her way to becoming a business woman. I give her a sheet to memorize which teaches her to carry on her dreams.

Many times I will have to remind them not to spend themselves out of business. By analogy I show them that should they open a dress shop, have a big sale, sell all their clothes, and spend the money, they would be out of business. So you have the same principle with your Mary Kay.

Recruiting Everywhere

I carry my recruiting materials with me on vacation, on planes—everywhere I go.

I recruited a girl on a plane flying out of Virginia one time. After spending two weeks' vacation, I boarded a plane in Bristol, Virginia. My seatmate was a lovely lady on her way to Hollywood, California.

My thoughts were: I have spent two whole weeks and not one person have I recruited. I turned to this lady and began talking with her, pulled out my recruiting materials from my attaché case and recruited her in just a few minutes. She said, "Thank God. I was just wondering what I would do when I return to Hollywood, because my husband works every day as superintendent of a factory, and I am alone all day." She had never had a facial.

I don't usually do this. I always see that a prospective recruit has a facial before she is recruited. But I called Susie Vickers, who lived in Hollywood, and had her give this girl a facial.

Another time I recruited a lady from Michigan in the aiport in Dallas while I was waiting for a plane connection. I could fill a book with my experiences of recruiting different places.

Make your contacts every place you go. For instance,

while visiting my son in Florida I was invited to a dinner. At this dinner I met a lovely lady and made an appointment the next day and recruited her.

In Pueblo, Colorado, standing in line in a cafeteria, I was introduced to a lady who was selling insurance. She began to try to recruit me to sell insurance. I out-talked her and made an appointment for that afternoon for her and her husband and recruited her that very evening.

On my way to Casper, Wyoming, I had a seat partner to whom I introduced myself, and that very night I had her in a class to recruit. Recruiting is an attitude; you must believe in your company wholeheartedly and you must believe in yourself. You must sell yourself. To recruit, you must sell all these things.

Here are some pointers on recruiting which I have shared with consultants before:

1. Shows—ask at least one from every show
   a. Four-point Recruiting Plan (study and know)
   b. Have plenty of recruiting info available to leave with prospects and hostesses
   c. Anticipate signing one recruit out of approximately every five shows
   d. Shows are one's best source
2. Friends (Isn't your recruiter a friend because she offered the opportunity to you?)
3. Pink Tickets
4. Third person approach
   a. This is what I'm looking for, can you help me find someone?
   b. Ask for referrals from everyone
      1) Customers
      2) Hostesses
      3) Business people
      4) Bankers
      5) Ministers

5. Cold Calling
   a. Carry recruiting info with you constantly
   b. "You should be doing what I do . . ."
   c. Book for facial with intent of recruiting immediately
6. Urgency
   a. Set deadline; believe it; act on it
   b. Waste no time
   c. Don't let indecision stall you. No decision is a "no" decision
   d. Set up appointments with idea of closing right then
7. Getting the interview (appointment)
   a. Excite and inspire
      1) Set the appointment the same as you would sell the Basic
         a. No obligation
         b. Want you to know the facts so you can make an intelligent decision
         c. Highlights only—what she most likely relates to
      2) Commissions vs. Hours

To recruit, you must ask. Jesus said in Matthew 7:7, "Ask and ye shall receive. Knock and it shall be opened unto you. Seek and ye shall find." Do you believe this? I do.

Ask everyone you think would be good. Ask customers for referrals. Seek, go after those hoping to help them. I often wonder what would have happened to me if no one had asked me. Just think what a wonderful life you can bring to them. I know and you should know by now that our company is the very best in the whole world. It really cares about the consultants. Our company shares its profits, shares its love. Our company really cares about us and loves us very much. It is a company that is fair in every respect.

Mary Kay even remembers every consultant on their birthday!

The product is the very best and if you don't really believe that, study it until you fall in love with it. Learn all about it and how to present it in a dignified, self-assured manner. Hold each jar in the same manner you would a diamond. Practice this until when you pick up a product, you will convey to your prospective customers your appreciation for each product.

Study yourself. Get rid of your hangups. Get rid of all prejudices, all procrastination. Develop a love for yourself so you can love others.

Stay calm when someone wrongs you. Remember they may be your next customer or recruit.

Recruiting is so simple. It only becomes hard when we make it that way—perhaps what we need is a reason to recruit. Here are just a few:

1. Recruiting makes you a better consultant.
2. Recruiting keeps your attitude positive.
3. You become a winner—and winning is fun!
4. Recruiting means added income for you and your recruit.
5. You can attain one of the greatest rewards your Mary Kay career offers—Directorship, and the privilege of helping others!

Well then, if it's so simple, why doesn't everyone recruit? Could it be that we need our thinking straightened out? Ask yourself two questions:

1. Do you decide that prospective recruits are not going to accept before you ask, so therefore, why ask?
2. Are you afraid that the prospective recruit can't succeed? If so, then ask yourself another question.

If you recruited someone who failed to become a Director, would you be the person responsible for all of her failures? NO! We can only offer the opportunity; she is responsible for the results.

Now if your thinking is straightened out, ask yourself some more questions:

1. Am I holding a minimum of three shows per week? The greatest number of recruits are found at shows. When you are holding shows, you stay excited and are willing to share with other people. You are in business when you are holding a minimum of three shows per week.

2. Am I excited about my career? Light a fire! Put a sparkle in your eyes. Be the kind of person that other people will want to be like. Be a ray of sunshine, not a cloud of doom.

3. Do I ask, or do I just think about it and never actually do it? Do I select the right people? Think about what this opportunity can mean to her—instead of what it means to you. Now, open your eyes and look at other Mary Kay consultants. Is there anyone who looks exactly like you? Okay then, does it matter if she has plenty of money or is broke; if she is married or single; outgoing or shy; young or middleaged; has two, three, four or five children or none; is a career girl or housewife; short or tall? Now look back to see if you have been judging people. Here are some traits you can look for: likes people, is people oriented, has good character, and good appearance.

4. Do I ask correctly? Sell her on the appointment to hear about our opportunity rather than the opportunity itself when you approach her. Don't let her make such an important decision without knowing the total picture. At a show, always talk privately to

the person you choose, or call back the next day and say, "I think you would enjoy doing what I do. Can we get together and talk about it?

5. Do you build her confidence while overcoming her objections? If she asks how much she can earn, tell her that this will be determined by the amount of time she puts into her career. She may ask, "How much do I have to invest?" Explain to her that there are several different ways she can begin her Mary Kay career and then explain these to her in simple terms. If she says, "I could never do anything like that." Tell her you know how she feels, (that you felt that way yourself) but did she notice how the product just sold itself! Explain to her that she will be taught everything she needs to know. She may say, "My husband won't let me." If so, you say, "I'm sure your husband wants you to be happy; perhaps he just doesn't understand what this is all about. Let's make an appointment at his convenience and let me tell him about it." Be prepared for objections—you usually have at least one objection to overcome before you get the appointment.

6. Do I follow through the prospective recruit? A prospective recruit remains a prospect for three days only! If she doesn't make her decision at the interview, tell her you will be back in touch within three days for her decision.

7. Do I have a plan on HOW to achieve my recruiting goals? For instance, your goal is to recruit four people this month, or to be a Gold Medal Winner and recruit five people this month. Do you have a minimum of seven shows booked (planning to hold five) each week during the month? Do you select one or two people from every show to ask?

Do you contact them within twenty-four hours to set up an appointment? Do you ask for the appointment in the right way and get definite appointments?

By correctly following each of these steps and then telling your prospective recruits about the fantastic Mary Kay opportunity, you should reach your recruiting goal!

Why should you recruit? You should recruit for profit.

If you recruit one consultant who sells $500 each month (and she will if you will share your responsibility as a recruiter and help her) you will make forty dollars per month on that one recruit. If you have eight recruits and if you have them selling $500 each month, this would give you $320 per month in recruit checks. Some consultants have made as high as $1,000 per month on recruits.

This is money in *your* pocket. it is out there; all you have to do is go after it. Commit yourself to sales, to sharing the opportunity, to your future, and the things that you personally can give to your family. Take a stand. Get the WINNING FEELING. You deserve the very best. Mary Kay offers all of this to you and you can have $1,000 in recruit bonus. We want you to and all you have to do is ask.

In I Corinthians 2:16 it says, "We have the mind of Christ in us." And I Corinthians 3:16 says the world is ours. Get out there with Christ's mind in yours and claim what he has given you!

Know where you are going, know what you want. Read Matthew 7:7 and *believe it.* Place yourself and all that concerns you lovingly in the Hands of God.

Never fear. Don't let doubts find a resting place in your mind. When you set a goal, decide then and there, that's it. We are studied in purpose, we are strengthened in spirit, and we are quiet and controlled in our emotions. God's spirit transforms every circumstance or condition. Be dedicated, don't get carried away with every whim that comes along. Don't let every person who has something to say use you. The Mary Kay Company has such a wonderful opportunity for me. I have a firm goal out there with my career and I want to reach it. I have never learned how to go in two different directions at once. You may say, "I set a goal but you just would not believe what has happened to me." Dr. Vincent Peale says he prays for problems. George Schuler says when you come to a mountain, just go through it.

As you invest your time, your life in your career, and in recruiting, you will grow and you will be more successful.

I had a pretty good success by mailing out a card to people in other towns. I had the telephone company mail me a telephone book for the nearby towns. Then at random, I selected names and addressed and mailed them this card:

MARY KAY COSMETICS INC. Would you be my talent scout? Mary Kay has asked me to locate outstanding women, like you, who might qualify to become beauty consultants. Think of someone who: 1. Enjoys people, 2. Likes helping others look beautiful, 3. Is fashion conscious, and 4. Last, but not least, enjoys making money. Put your thinking cap on and call me as soon as you think of someone. Call Collect! I will give you ten dollars for each person that *you get that comes in*. Thanks, Mary McDowell, Director, 2208 Salinas, Odessa, TX 337-1412.

I highly recommend you follow up with phone calls to get the best results.

Here's another method to try that helps in winning recruits. Try this contest. I sent out letters like this:

START-LOOK-LISTEN! Contest

The word for this month beginning the 1st through 27th. Read all about the MCDOWELL RECRUITING CONTEST. Everyone can be a WINNER! Contest is from 1st to 27th. All orders in by midnight.

Contest Rules, Regulations & Prizes

One new recruit	$ 10 Bonus Prize
Two new recruits	$ 20 Bonus Prize
Three new recruits	$ 35 Bonus Prize
Four new recruits	$ 60 Bonus Prize
Five new recruits	$100 Bonus Prize

Definition of what constitutes a recruit in contest: One new consultant with $500 wholesale order in means 1 recruit. One new consultant with under $250 wholesale orders in, 1/2 recruit. One new consultant with $1,000 order means two recruits. In other words, a new recruit with under $250 wholesale order in counts as 1/2 recruit. Any questions? Write or call me.

The McDowell Unit is on its way
To hit the Top with Mary Kay.
With recruiting teamwork, we won't stop
Until we're there, at the very top.

To spur us on, I'm willing to pay
Recruiting money every day.
Two gets you twenty, one gets you ten
Thirty-five for three, ya come alive?
Sixty dollars is yours when you get four
And five will win you forty more.

Mediocrity is not our name,
Our new recruits will win the game.
Tho in the past we might have blundered
Let's get FIVE and win the HUNDRED.

One for the money, two for the shooting
Get ready, get set, to start recruiting.

The starting gun will go off at midnight, the 1st.

Good luck to all and may God bless.
Your Director,
Mary

A Recruit Manual

I made a recruit manual. I do believe this is the most important tool to recruit with.

I took a photo album. On the front I put the prettiest picture I could find of Mary Kay. I cut out flowers from a Hallmark card and surrounded her with flowers.

I told how Mary Kay started the company, that her philosophy is God first, family second, and your Mary Kay career third. I tell about her guarantee. I talk about her beauty, her beautiful life.

On the second page I have pictures of our big vans that carry our products to the branch offices. On the same two pages I list the branch offices locations. On the third page I have pictures of our president and vice presidents and talk about how wonderful they are. In short, I do a good selling job on our company.

On the fourth page, Mary Kay presents to you a golden opportunity. The fifth page is a map drawn of the entire U.S.A. The entire country is your territory. No one can squeeze you out. The sixth page shows "shorter hours." Self-fulfillment: You can be among the stars.

Seventh page emphasizes low overhead, because you work out of your home. Life-time security: Your success is geared to your own ambitions. You can make as little money or as much as you want. There is no ceiling on your earnings.

You have an educational opportunity in "We Study How To Improve Our Attitudes." You can be a Mary Kay Director in six months. Eighth page: Our company is reliable. Our product is superior. You are your own boss. We are not your boss. We are only your business advisors. We learn makeup. Makeup is an art. We say you have money to spend for anything you want and that is beautiful.

The ninth page tells of tax benefits. Your home: Do you own your home, or are you buying and making monthly payments? Do you rent furnished, perhaps? You take a portion of your home, your lights, water, gas, insurance, depreciation, all off your taxes, because your office is in your home. Your maid who cleans your office, or your telephone, if it is a business phone. Child care: $200 for each child. Everything connected with one car—or eighteen cents per mile. Take your case and deduct forty-four dollars every day you are out. All travel expenses, food and cleaning while you are away.

You can start with a $62.25 case and make more money than I did when I started in Mary Kay. For example, suppose your husband started to school to be a dentist. He would have to go to school seven years, and in two years you will be making more money than he will when he finishes dental school, and he will still have to have an office that would cost him at least $20,000 to set up.

If you were to think of going into business, you probably would first think of a dress shop. A dress shop would cost you at least $22,000 to start. A laundry, $10,000. A cleaners, $10,000. If you become a dentist, it would cost you $22,000 and that would not buy your books.

Should you open a store, you would need something to sell. You will be going into business when you join Mary Kay and you will be president of your own company. So you will need products to sell. You will have to have a working case which costs $65 plus tax. Mary Kay at this time lets a girl start with what we call a fast start for $200. This gives you $400 worth of products retail.

If you possibly can order $400 wholesale you will get $65 worth of products free—enough to pay for your case. You probably have that much in savings or checking accounts. If you do, borrow it from yourself. If you don't, borrow it from the bank and set it up to pay off at fifty dollars per month. This way it won't bother your budget in any way. You do have a checking account, don't you? You don't? Well, we will go another way. You do have your home, don't you? You do have your furniture, your car, television, anything you own you can borrow the money on. If you go the $200 route, you will need to borrow enough for your case, your order and the tax.

I then show the avenues of income or the Mackilany plan. I lay down my manual and look straight into their eyes and say, "Now what do you think?" If they don't have anything to put up for security, no money, no credit, I find they are poor prospects for recruits. I have tried to help them, but find they are more of a liability than anything else.

Responsibility to Recruits

Take note: Mary Kay does not give us that recruit check for nothing.

It is our responsibility to take those recruits as if they were our own children. Remember, we lead them to invest their hard earned money and we are responsible for that consultant's getting a return on her money as we told her she would. You owe it to her to be an example in recruiting and selling. I have never asked one of my consultants to do anything that I was not willing to do myself. Mary Kay says, "The speed of the leader is the speed of the gang."

For instance, I learned a great lesson one morning while out in my garden. I was pulling some weeds out of my beautiful flowers. Down covered up with the other flowers, I found a big, healthy plant smothered by the other plants and it could not grow. I dug it up, carried it to another spot in my garden and I thought, I will put some Rapid Grow on you and watch you grow. I imagined how beautiful it would be.

I went into the house and something drew my thoughts away from the flowers. Some time later in the day, I went back out through my garden and found my beautiful plant withered and drooped, almost dead. At once my mind went to our recruits and I thought, "That's what happens to our recruits when we neglect to give them what they need."

We recruit them and think, "My, she is going to be great." We have our teaching class turn her loose, expecting her to go to the top. What happens? She goes out, has a show that is not as big as we pictured for her when we recruited her. She probably gets on the phone as we taught her and no one books. Let's face it: not everyone books that first call. Many times we book them four or five times before they hold. In our rush we didn't tell her that. So she folds just like the flower because it was not firmly rooted and nurtured.

That recruit will be ready to send back her product because she thinks she is not the type to sell. Whose fault is it? Ours, of course. In our mind's eye, we saw her fully bloomed when she was just a recruit and yet we have failed to supply the things she needed to make her bloom.

I am guilty and I am quite sure that you are too.

I am the only director in our town. Many, many consultants call me and say I have just recruited into Mary Kay and have never had one little bit of training. Could you help me? I always take them gladly and do by them as I do by my own consultants. But deep down in my mind I tell myself that that person who recruited the girl should at least try to train her by mail or write me a short note once in a while and say, "Mary, I appreciate what you are doing for my consultant." I had the joy recently of having a DIQ call and tell me how much she appreciated me for taking the time to train her from the very first facial.

She talked for a solid hour. I spent many hours with her when she was down and I cheered her along. When she was high, I praised her! She would call long distance to tell me she was low or had a problem or a big show. I always had time to help her. Now she was through her DIQ training. I was getting the honors for her success that should by all rights have gone to her recruiter. She had come in on a plane and had called from the airport to tell me. She had just spent a week in Dallas and she didn't even wait till she got home to tell me what my training had done for her. She had never been shown one single thing by her recruiter or director and had driven sixty-five miles to come to my sales meeting instead. I felt good about helping her. How about the person who recruited her?

Let's wake up, girls. When we take someone out of their way of life and place them in this company, let's not get so busy we let them die for need of more attention.

I sincerely believe if I could go back and have all the girls I have recruited to train again, I would retain many more than I have. Let's resolve together from this day forward to see that our consultants are more knowledgeable in every way so that when they go out in the field and face difficulties, they won't wilt and die like that flower in my garden but will bloom and grow and flourish.

I have noticed so many times when the recruiter starts failing, her recruit most often will fail. We owe it to them to hang in there. We have responsibilities to those we recruit.

RECRUITER'S RESPONSIBILITIES

After Interview:

1. Furnish new recruit with a manual and see that she gets the questionnaire filled in.
2. Arrange for her to observe three shows.
3. Tell her how to get her first eight to ten shows booked . . . in detail.
4. Help her fill out her first order . . . (to be placed with application).
5. See that she has rubber stamp made and sends for gold stickers.
6. Review her training schedule (given to her by her Director), and help her follow it. She must get Director's permission to change dates.
7. Be sure she attends training class.
8. Help her get beauty case ready for first show, including filling artist pallete, etc.
9. Help her arrange her merchandise for shows.
10. Show her how to *clean* beauty case. This *MUST* be done properly and thoroughly.
11. Call her first eight to ten hostesses. Thank them for helping the new recruit get started in her new

career—COACH THEM and rebook if necessary with definite date.

12. Help new recruit set up goals—short and long range.

13. Have new recruit call you after *each* of her first week's shows. Answer all questions that have arisen at each show and *encourage* her!

14. Arrange for new recruit to attend sales meeting *every week!* Have her block off her sales meeting time in her date book for the first six weeks. (Shows do *not* constitute an excused absence.) *Tell* her and *show* her by example that there is to be NO NEGATIVISM at sales meetings!!!

CHAPTER VII

BASICS FOR SUCCESSFUL SELLING

A Candid Look at Self

My first step I had to take was to establish a purpose for myself . . . what did I want out of my Mary Kay career?

My next step was to build an image for my company and myself. My identity was very important to me. I wanted people to say, "That's Mary McDowell; she's a Mary Kay cosmetics salesperson!" I wanted people to see a lady who was professional, well-dressed, who stood out in a crowd, a person whom everyone loved—a person whom people would look at when she walked through a door at the restaurant—one whom people trusted, or that everyone liked to be with. My first job was to work me over!

I had a special company to represent, a special product, to present, and I had to be a special person to everyone. So I had to be worked over. My nails had to be cared for, my hands had to have some attention, but most of all, I had to get my real me straightened out.

Some experiences came my way to help me find myself. I would like to relate them to you. Perhaps it will help you avoid some pitfalls.

One day a call came on the phone from a girl who wanted some Mary Kay delivered to her place of work.

The place was a lousy bar, one of the very lowest to be found, and I knew it. My grandson was standing by when she called and I turned to him and said, "The only way I will deliver this is for you to go with me." He said, "Yes, I will go with you." On the way, he turned to me and said, "Now, Granny, when we get to this bar, we are not going to see smoke falling from the ceiling." When I arrived I found one of the most precious girls I have ever met. At this point I began to try to understand why some girls worked in bars. Then later I had a call to carry food to a needy family. When I arrived, I found a young mother with ten children to support. When I asked her where she worked, she told me she worked in a bar. Then she explained, "I don't want to work in a bar, but I have no education and this is the only way I can support my children and keep them from starving."

My attitude started changing about people. Then in a few days, I booked a show with a lady and when I arrived she had her guests there, but the house was piled from one room to the other. The floor was cluttered, her dishes were piled high in the sink. I had to push dishes around to get to the water to wet my wash cloths. But I had some good sales and left that house with money and mixed emotions.

I had learned that this woman was a Brownie scout leader and gave just about all of her time to her troop. Her house being cluttered didn't bother her so why should it bother me?

I had taken a new recruit with me to observe the show. This recruit had placed a $500 order that morning. When we left the show, I dropped her off at her home and just as I entered my home, the phone was ringing. Pope McDonald, our national sales director, was on the phone asking me why my recruit had called and cancelled her order. I was greatly disturbed and got in touch with my new recruit and learned she didn't want to work with dirty housekeepers. I straightened her out and through this experience, I learned to accept people of all walks of life, just as they are.

I learned I was not a judge of morals or conduct. I was a beauty consultant and my job was to make people think more of themselves and pray that they might change their way. My job was to make myself better, to think pure thoughts, and dwell on the good that is in people and look for that good. And would you believe when I started to look at my faults and failures and looking for the good in everyone, my whole life changed. I had been a Christian for many years and had given of myself and my time. All these years I had looked down my nose, so to speak, at others all this time. I had searched for the bad in their lives and overlooked the good.

Another thing I had to change was the determination I had built within myself through the years that my point of view was right. I hated to admit I was wrong about things. I can now say very graciously, "I am so sorry; I was wrong."

I also hated to admit I had made a mistake about things. This had to change. You see, I had a big job—working on me.

It suddenly began to dawn on me that this job was tremendous. I had to have some help in making me over. I had to have help but where was I going to get that help? Why, Jesus, of course. So I took Him then and there at that moment as my business partner and you know what He did? He did it all for me. The minute I made my decision, that I wanted to be a better person, He came to my rescue.

I started reading my Bible every morning and praying and then I would turn my business over to God. I started believing God's world was full of abundance. I believed His world was rich with potential and possibilities. I believed goals were met, that success was achieved, that dreams did come true.

I believed the world was overflowing with blessings. I believed God wanted us to prosper. That this was His plan if I would only meet the conditions. I believed He could take a sixty-three-year-old woman and make her successful.

I believed that there was not anything we could not accomplish after being put in God's hand. Mark 11:23: "Whoever believes that what he says will come to pass, it will be done for him." He would always assure me I could do it.

I began to believe that I could recruit, that I could sell. I realized my handicaps. I realized it was not wise for me to be out driving so I had to devise another plan—do it in my home.

After probing deep into the recesses of my heart, I learned I was so anxious to reach the top, I had a tiny bit of jealousy in my heart. I knew this had to go.

Then I remembered the experience in Bristol of the lights going out. Through the months and years of working constantly on me as I learned my Mary Kay work, I remembered how I took common clay and made a beautiful slipper.

I Peter 5:7, "Cast all your anxieties on him; for he cares about you."

The following credo expresses my feelings about the power of belief:

The deepest ocean—the tallest mountain, the most powerful animal cannot believe. Only man can believe. The height of man's success is determined by the depth of his belief.

WE BELIEVE the immutable laws of the universe positively state that man reaps what he sows. That opportunity carries responsibility, example is the best teacher, and fair play seeks what is right—not who is right.

WE BELIEVE sweat on the brow from honest labor is one of life's most glorious sights and to show your fellow man the dignity and value of work is to increase his stature and self worth. That real satisfaction comes from total effort fully expended in quest of a worthy ideal.

WE BELIEVE self-acceptance and personal growth combined with honesty and loyalty give a man the inner peace and strength necessary for success and happiness. That character, faith, and integrity are the foundations for greatness and the man who doesn't stand for something will fall for anything.

WE BELIEVE Jesus Christ was speaking to you and to me when He said, "What I have done—ye can do also—and more." That man was created in God's own image and is designed for acomplishment, engineered for success, and endowed with the seeds of greatness. Believing these things, we neither look down nor up to any man.

WE BELIEVE unconditional love-giving and forgiving—is the vital ingredient in man's search for meaning. That to live is to love, to love is to help, and to help is to understand the difference between a hand and a handout. That you can get everything in life you want if you help other people get what they want.

BECAUSE WE BELIEVE—and love—our purpose in life is to help you—help yourself!*

Activation of Attitudes

Your attitude is what makes the difference in your business. "You can do everything right with the wrong

*Source unknown

attitude and fail, and everything wrong with the right attitude and succeed." How many times would you say you have heard this saying? You will continue to hear it over and over again as long as you are with Mary Kay because it is so true! When they begin their careers, most consultants spend too much time worrying about their knowledge of the products or their techniques. These things will all come in time. The most important thing to concentrate on is your attitude. For if your attitude is a negative one, you will give up before you have a chance to learn the details of your business.

Attitude affects everything you do. It affects your shows, your sales, your bookings. But with the right attitude you can make something good come of every seemingly bad happening. I truly believe you can't have a "bad" show. You may have a show with low sales, but if you did your best, made someone there feel good about herself and had a chance to practice your presentation, how could it be bad?

Don't even let the words "I can't" sink into your thinking. I have never allowed myself to say "I can't." There are a few times I say, "I haven't done this before," but never "I can't." Stop yourself the next time you are tempted to make an excuse for why you haven't been doing what you would like to do. Be honest with yourself! If you lie to yourself often enough, you will start to believe it. When you have a few shows that cancel, don't let your attitude become one of, "Well, I'll have two shows this week if they don't cancel on me." Maybe you didn't coach well enough or possibly you didn't excite your hostess sufficiently. Take better precautions against cancellations or ask your director for advice on how to prevent them, but don't begin expecting the worst.

When you have a prospective recruit that terminates, don't give up recruiting and say, "It's not for me." That's taking the easy way out. Never asking means never being rejected, but it also means you'll never go where you want to go. I personally have recruited many consultants who didn't stay with the company as long as I have, but I never felt like a failure. You never fail until you quit.

Booking is another area that seems to be so easy for some and so hard for others. I really believe the ones who have no trouble with booking are those whose attitude is, "How can I help this person?" instead of, "I really need a $100 show." It is true that the way you ask has a great deal to do with the results you get, but you must be open-minded and learn from those with more experience than you. Sales is an occupation that is learned and not something that just happens. When you go to your weekly sales meetings, remember that it is time to get your battery recharged and your confidence rebuilt. You must come willing to listen and be affected by the success of others. You'll go home feeling that you can do all the things those superstars are doing! Never come to a sales meeting to express the negative feeling you may have inside. Come and let someone else's positive feeling into your head and heart. If you can truly be excited when things are bad, imagine what it will be like when things are good!

From now on, make a promise to yourself that you will never say "I can't."

Now believe: Everything good that happens to me, I initiate; or it starts in my mind. The Bible says, "As a man thinketh, so is he." I believe this.

From the first day I started to sell Mary Kay products, I never left the house for a show that I did not carry six boxes filled as completely as possible. When I left the house, I knew in my mind that those six boxes would never see my door again. Because I was going to sell them. And usually I did. I always sell five out of six at least—and sometimes the sixth also.

When I begin my shows, I talk with the guests just like they have already bought the product. I say, "Now, Mary, tonight when you clean your face, you do this and this . . ." I drift on around the table and say to Jane, "Now Jane, tonight when you clean your face, you do this or that. . . ." I say this same thing during the show to each guest.

When I close my show, I always say, "Now let me run over this again so you will know how to use your product and how simple it is." What I am really doing is getting their attention completely on the product. If you don't, they won't buy.

I say, "You clean your face with the cleansing cream and put on the freshener and a small amount of night cream. Now feel your wrist that has the night cream and the one that does not." They always say, "What a difference." I have had them even feel the wrong one and say there is so much difference! I then say, "You put the freshener and Day Radiance on. Use your masque twice each week. This is your basic."

"This is the Lip-Eye pallette. It is made out of the same material as your telephone. It has two sable brushes and these refills are removable. You now have a wardrobe of color you can carry in your purse. This mascara will not run; you can cry, go swimming, and it won't run. This rouge will last you five years, or you may prefer the blush. This is your complete skin care and glamour program. Let's see, now, you want it all, don't you?"

I had to go to the next one and say the same, "You want it all, don't you?" If one of the six says, "I believe I will just take the basic." I act just as happy as if she had bought the whole complete set and then book her to get the Glamour. I usually say, "I have three ways you can buy this: you can pay me cash in full with money or a check, or you can pay me half and pay the other in two weeks, or you can pay it out." I don't have layaways.

I have envelopes printed with my name and address on them and give them envelopes to mail their payments to me. Another thing I do all the time I am giving the facial is say, "My, you are looking good. One would hardly believe you would look this much better. Just look at yourself. Why, your eyes are just shining."

I am telling them the truth. Remember you sell what you sell, always.

Remember when you booked the show, you had to sell the appointment; then you had to tie the appointment down or you would not have had the show.

Here is a Self-Confidence Creed that I find helpful and offer to others for their personal commitment:

I believe in myself. I believe in those who work with me. I believe in my employer. I believe in my friends. I believe in my family. I believe that God will lend me everything I need with which to succeed if I do my best to earn it through faithful and honest service. I believe in prayer and I will never close my eyes to sleep without praying for divine guidance to the end that I will be patient with other people and tolerant with those who do not believe as I do.

I believe that success is the result of intelligent effort and does not depend upon luck or sharp practice or double crossing friends, fellow men, or my employer. I believe I will get out of life exactly what I put into it; so, I'll be careful to conduct myself toward others as I would want them to act toward me. I will not slander those whom I do not like. I will not slight my work no matter what I may see others doing. I will render the best service of which

I am capable because I have pledged myself to succeed in life, and I know that success is always the result of conscientious and efficient effort. Finally, I will forgive those who offend me because I realize that I shall sometimes offend others and I will need their forgiveness. *

Let me suggest how to change your life from a negative attitude to a positive attitude:

The first step is to discover your own negative self and admit to yourself you are negative.

Second is to start looking at your negative points and replace them with positive feelings.

Do you see yourself as a vibrant, exciting person full of vivid impressions and new experiences? Or do you see yourself a depressed, unhappy person? If you are a negative person, start today to make yourself over. Begin by loving yourself. Then love others. You must first love yourself before you can love other people. When doubt creeps in, push it out of your mind.

When the thought comes into your mind that someone is not the right kind of person, replace that thought with something good about them. When fear creeps in, repeat the 23rd Psalm as fast as you can. When the thought creeps in that you may not succeed, go to repeating these lines to yourself over and over: "What the mind can conceive, you can achieve."

When someone says anything about someone that is not good, quickly say something good about them.

Go into your bedroom, look into the mirror and repeat these words: "I can be successful. I will be successful. I cannot fail. I will go to the top. I will practice, practice." Before many weeks you will become a

* Source unknown

positive person and will hate the thought of negativism.

No one can change your attitude but you. You are in the driver's seat. I can assure you that you will become a happier person with positive attitudes. You will have more friends and will sell more products. Just stay away from negative people. I might add that also you will be healthier than when you were negative. Wake up and live the good life. Be positive about everything. Should you run into a mountain, go over it or through it.

I heard Dr. Vincent Peale say one time, "If you don't have any problems, get down on your knees and say, 'Oh, Lord, send me some problems.' " The reason is this: When you have problems and solve them, you are a bigger, better person than before.

I learned early in my Mary Kay career if I wanted to be a winner I had to make things happen.

Mary Kay said one day to keep your shelves full of product and you would go out and sell it. These words stayed in my memory. My first step to make things happen was to keep a big stock at all times. When things were not happening fast for me, I would go into my Mary Kay room and rearrange my product. By doing this I knew full well I would have to get some shows going. I would immediately go to the phone and book shows. My mind would work overtime on how to sell the product.

If I didn't get all the bookings I needed, I would dress up, go to town smiling at everyone I met, saying hello to all my friends. Before many words were exchanged, the conversation would turn to Mary Kay. I usually carried a Mary Kay bag, wore a Mary Kay pin or my Diamond Bee. These nearly always did the trick of bringing up the subject; and before they realized it, I would have a show booked.

I also learned if I wanted to be a winner I had to keep motivated each day. I did this many ways. One way was I would go into my room I like so much, close the door, and play a motivation tape or read a motivation book such as *Think and Grow Rich* by Napoleon Hill; *Dynamic Laws of Prosperity* by Katherine Ponder; *Psycho-Pictography* by Vernon Howard; *As a Man Thinketh* by James Allen; *Unlock Your Faith Power* by Vincent Peale.

Another lesson I learned early was if I wanted to be a winner I had to keep my mind on my goal and give my time to my business.

We must remember our Mary Kay business is big business and we must treat it as big business. I have always taken my Mary Kay career seriously.

Sure there are many things I like to do—sewing is one of the things I love to do so much. Sewing does for me what gold does for some people. Painting china is another one of my hobbies. I love it very much, just as I also love painting pictures with oil. I also love to can and cook, grow flowers, go to parties and all sorts of socials. I soon learned I could not do these things as much and be a winner as I wanted.

Being on that stage in Queens Court and being Queen gave me the greatest joy of my life. I wanted this to prove to myself that I could do it. I also learned if I wanted to be a winner, I had to sell products, lots of products.

In order to sell products, I needed people. So I did everything in my power to make friends with every person I met—both men, women, and children. I knew I had to love everyone, so my big job was to ignore anything anyone said that I didn't like and to develop an understanding of people—what made them act the way they do.

The hardest lesson I learned was to forgive everyone for anything they said about me, especially if it happened to be false. I knew that to be a winner I had to forgive because I know God could not bless me and make me a winner if I had malice, jealousy, or hatred in my heart.

CHAPTER VIII

BETTER BOOKING

Creative Strategies

Booking is the lifeline of our business.

If you will learn to book well, you will always have great sales. Study everything you can find on booking. Try different ways to book. I have listed some ways for you to use. Start with enthusiasm. If you don't have it, get it before you start. Try these suggestions:

1. *Thank God in Advance.* Say, "Thank you, Lord, for the bookings you are going to bless me with today."

2. *Customer Service.* When calling pink tickets and your customer orders quite a lot, say to her, "Listen, Sally, I just really don't want to sell you this product, I want to GIVE it to you. I'm sure you have at least three friends you would like to share our marvelous Skin Care Program with . . . ."

3. *Business Cards.* Never take a receipt, change, etc., that you don't place a business card in that cashier's hand. Always leave your card on top of your tip in a restaurant. Leave your card in ladies' rooms, beauty salons, doctors' offices, laundromats, etc. Put a card in every bill you mail out monthly and spray the envelope with our cologne. Every outside order you sack—put a card in it. Give everyone at your shows and facials a business card.

4. Wear your *MARY KAY PIN UPSIDE DOWN*. Thank you! That's to remind me to ask if you have had your Mary Kay facial.

5. *Gold Labels.* Carry them in your purse. While sitting in doctors' offices, etc., put a gold label on every magazine cover.

6. *Play Games with Yourself.* Have a scavenger hunt—go out and book groups of people for a facial—such as people who wear white uniforms, nurses, secretaries, grandmother, etc. Tell them you are in the area offering free facials to every person you meet wearing a white uniform. Or, call some of your friends and tell them that next week is Grandmother's Week and you are trying to book as many grandmothers as possible. Ask them if they would give you the name of their grandmother. Just decide on a group (teachers, clerks, waitresses, etc.) and then go out and book them.

7. *Facial Boxes.* Put a little sign up that reads, "If you're not becoming to him—you should be coming to me!"

Why should you continually direct book? 1. To fill your datebook, 2. To get new chains going, 3. To get back on the books, 4. To rebuild your self-confidence, 5. To find recruits.

Where & Who? 1. Beauty Shops, 2. Doctor and Dentist offices, 3. Cleaners, 4. Dairy Queens—Restaurants, 5. Church, 6. PTA, 7. Neighbors—invite over for coffee, 8. Clerks, 9. Bank Tellers, 10. Grocery Clerks—(You may say something like this: "I've been coming here for weeks and have been meaning to ask you, have you had your complimentary facial with Mary Kay?")

How to book and what to say:

1. Look the part—dress professionally with bag and corsage if you wish.

2. Smile. Expect a YES and project enthusiasm with sparkling eyes and an alert attitude. Be the type of person you'd be interested in knowing. A beautiful woman is one you notice. A charming woman is one that notices you.

3. Strike up a conversation. Get them to talking—weather, children—ask questions about them. Make it casual. Don't be overpowering, loud, or conspicuous. You may say, "By the way, may I ask you a question? Have you had your complimentary facial with Mary Kay?' If she says, "No, I haven't," you may say "What type of complexion do you have—oily, dry, combination, sensitive? We specialize in skin care and our products are designed to normalize the skin conditions. I would love to be the one to give you your complimentary facial and get your opinion. When is your day off? When would be a good time for us to get together?" (Give a choice.) If she's busy say, "Let me give you my card with name and phone number, and may I have yours. I'll call you tonight and we'll set up a convenient date and time."

4. If she says, "Yes, I have and didn't like it, or it broke me out" say, "Oh, I'm so sorry to hear that, that's so unusual. Most people who try it love it and get good results. (Hand her your card.) I'd like to give you my card and if any time in the future you need my services, feel free to call me."

5. For those who approach you (bag or corsage)—"Oh, I'm so glad that you asked. I'm a Mary Kay consultant and we attended a convention in Dallas. Have you had your facial with Mary Kay?"

6. Turn your conversations around to Mary Kay. While shopping for a dress, say to the clerk, "Do you

think this is appropriate for a show?" Or, "I need something that is washable."

Make direct and telephone booking a part of your day-to-day living. Add at least three such bookings to your datebook a day. But remember, show booking is the best and most dependable because: 1. Your Hostess is your business partner, 2. Your Hostess has had the facial and is enthusiastic, 3. You've had the opportunity to coach her, and 4. You have a tie with her from your Former Hostess.

Another tip is to SEND THANK YOU CARDS. Dear Mrs. Jones: Thank you for giving me the opportunity of introducing you to Mary Kay Cosmetics. I'm looking forward to seeing you at (time and date). Remember to invite your friends to share your facial time.

Remember to book in close. You'll get some no's, but one YES is worth ten no's.

Booking shows and facials contest:

1. We could give something FREE to everyone who will come to our house for a facial. (Such as a fifteen cent or twenty cent gift.) This should make booking easier.

2. Have a contest, or rather a drawing, on a set date. Everyone who has a facial at this house puts her name in the drawing box and the winner at the drawing gets a choice of a steak knife or some other prize worth two dollars or so.

3. From now until (set a date), we have another drawing. Everyone who comes to your house for a facial gets her name in the box. If they bring a friend, they get to put in their name twice and the friend also gets to enter. There is no limit to the number of people they can recruit for facials. Every person they bring gets to enter.

4. We've got to think up a good prize for the next year's drawing. A suggestion from me would be a choice

of a rhinestone watch, value $50; or a prize that you yourself have won from Mary Kay of approximate value.

Ideas for Booking Shows

During my years of selling, I have developed sound practical ways for increasing bookings. Some of these are listed below:

I

Pick up the phone directory and select ten names. Call and say: "Mrs. Doe, this is _____. I am a Mary Kay consultant and would like to take a minute of your time. May I?" (pause) "Have you had a Mary Kay facial? Have you seen Mary Kay on TV? Do you use a skin care program? What do you use?" If she says "I use Estee Lauder," say, "Oh, that's a great product. I would appreciate it so much if you would give me your opinion of Mary Kay. If I gave you a facial, would you give me your opinion of it? When would you like to have it, this week or next?"

II

Dress up your hair; fix your nails; no slacks; go into some store, grocery, department, or drug store. Select some nice looking lady. Walk over as if you were trying to decide what to get. If it is a grocery store, say "Lady, would you please tell me what you think of this bleach? Have you ever used it? Oh, thank you so much. By the way, I am _____ and I am with Mary Kay Cosmetics, and I am a trained beauty consultant. You have been so nice to me, I would like to do something for you. Could I give you a free Mary Kay facial?" Book the facial and turn it into a show.

Go to another store, do the same thing. Keep circulating around booking shows in the same manner until you have a full week's booking.

III

Drive into a filling station and ask the operator to give you five gallons of gas. I have a lock on my gas tank. I also have a shield on my license plates saying "Mary Kay." I say, "Would you mind, please, to look and see if I still have my shield on my license plate?" When he comes back, I say, "By the way, are you married?" If he says "Yes" I say, "Do you know if your wife uses Mary Kay or not?" If he says she does not, then say, "Would you mind if I call her and give her a free facial?" If he says he doesn't mind, you get her phone number and call her and say, "Mrs. _____, I have just bought some gas from your husband and he thought you might like a free Mary Kay facial."

When you leave that station, go to another and repeat your performance, another, and another until your tank is full and you will have four facials to give.

IV

Call a telephone number and say, "Is this so and so? Oh, I am so sorry. Will you forgive me for bothering you. By the way, have you had a Mary Kay facial? You haven't? I would love to give you one to repay you for bothering you. When would you like to get it?" When she books, turn it into a show.

V

Dress up, no slacks, hair fixed, nails manicured. Go to a shopping center. When you see some nice girl with glasses on, say, "By the way, I am on a scavenger hunt. My Director sent me out this morning with instructions that I was to offer every really pretty girl who wore glasses a free facial, and I think you are a very beautiful girl. So when would you like to get your facial?"

Repeat this until you have all the bookings you need. Turn the facial into a show, of course.

VI

When you go into a restaurant for a meal and the waitress brings the check, whisper to her and say, "Honey, you have been so nice to me, I want to do something for you. I want to give you a free Mary Kay facial. When you book her, turn it into a show.

VII

There's a saying, "You can find a man a fish and he'll eat for a day. But teach a man to fish and he'll eat for a lifetime."

Go fishing yourself. You may catch a suggestion from others. Try the following note to your representatives:

Dear consultants, I have listed for you many ways to book and to sell. Will you select one of these ideas and use it for two weeks and write and tell me what you think of them. Did they work for you?

Do you have a selling idea that I have not listed? If you do, please mail it to me.

VIII

Compound your bookings through a creative use of your current bookings. Remember: Their bookings are actually yours also.

1. When you book a facial and sell the customer, as she starts to leave, say, "Mrs. Doe, I have a plan whereby you can receive that lovely Intrigue Cologne

you selected as your favorite, absolutely free. Call ten of your friends and tell them how much you liked your facial and that you would be delighted to call me and arrange a facial for them. When the tenth one comes, whether she buys or not, I will present you with a bottle of Intrigue Cologne."

2. Call all your customers and say, "Mrs. Doe, I do appreciate you so much as a customer. And I respect your judgment. So, I want to make a suggestion to you. I would love to have you for a preferred customer. This is what you would do. I will bring you some shampoo, conditioner, lip pallettes, mascara, hair spray, pencil liners, and blushes for you to show and sell to your friends, and for any orders you can pick up from those who have had facials and bought products, I will give you twenty percent on everything you sell. You would like this, would you not?"

Go to apartment managers, if they are women, and offer them the same opportunity.

3. Another idea that has worked for me. Call your customers for that second facial and say, "Mrs. Doe, it is time for your second facial. If you will bring two of your friends with you, I will give you a bottle of our lovely lotion. You now have three people, which make a show. Three people and fifty dollars is a show and if you don't sell fifty dollars from three people, you will need to go back to the manual and study your product some more.

4. This is a great idea. This is called the 51 club. You write down on a page of paper numbers one to seventeen and draw lines for each number. When you book a show, say "Mrs. Doe, I have a good idea for you. Take this page with seventeen lines. Sell at least $3.00 to someone for each number, putting her name on the line, and fill this completely up. And when I come for my show, I will let you draw from these lines one name who

will receive a lovely gift from me and you will have anywhere from five to ten dollars hostess credit at retail price for yourself.

Don't you think this would be great?"

5. While giving a facial, I ask the customer if she is married. A little further along during the facial, I ask her where her husband works. I jot this down. When her facial is completed, I fill out her order and ask her when her birthday is—the day and the month, not the year. And tell when she has a birthday, she can order anything she wants at ten percent discount anytime during the month. I then ask her for her husband's name. I usually say, "Would you please give me your anniversary date?" During the facial I have demonstrated all three colognes, bath, and jell. I now say, "Mrs. Doe, which cologne have you decided you like best?" When she tells me, I jot it down on her profile case. Also, her anniversary and her husband's name. I now have the information I need to serve this customer all through the year.

When she has a birthday, I send her a card or call and remind her she can buy at ten percent discount. I then call her husband and say, "Mr. Doe, I thought you might like for me to remind you that your wife has a birthday this week. And I thought you might appreciate it if I told you she likes the Angel Fire Cologne so much. And I would be glad to wrap the present and deliver it to her for you."

Then when Christmas comes I call him and sell him a set of Angel Fire and Bath Powder. When Valentine's Day comes, I call and sell him Angel Fire Bath Jell. Then Mother's Day, I call him again and tell him his wife should be ready for another bottle of cologne. Then when her anniversary comes up, I do the same.

I now am really servicing my customer and I am

building confidence in the husband and by now he is depending on me to take care of his gifts for him. And I am building my business at the same time. This husband will feel grateful to me for helping his solve his gift problems.

Using Facial Boxes

Facial boxes can be very good sources for getting bookings.

I want to give you an example how well one paid off for me. I put out facial boxes when I first started my career and needed bookings. One was placed in a Gulf filling station. A sixteen-year-old boy put his name in the box just for fun. After picking up the box and calling those who had registered for a free facial, I ran into Johnny's name. I placed a call to his home knowing full well he would be in school. This is the way I handled it.

"Mrs. _____, is Johnny there? Please may I speak with him?" His mother answered, "Why no, he is in school. Could I take a message?" To which I answered, "Mrs. _____, I am a Mary Kay consultant and have a facial box out at the service station on the corner and Johnny registered for a facial. Would you like to get it?" To which she replied, "Yes."

I then said, "Would you like for me to come to your house or you come to mine?" She said, "I would like for you to come to my home." "When would you like to have your facial, first part of the week or last?" She said, "I believe the first." I then asked if Tuesday morning would be a good time and she said, "Yes." Then I continued, "Mrs. _____, I could give two or three facials just as easily as I can yours alone. Do you have a couple of friends who would like to have a facial free? She replied that she believed she did. So I then said, "By the way, if you could have six people, I would give them all facials; and if they buy any products you might get yours free, if you like the product." "Oh, that would be great," she said.

I went to her home, had the show, and sold $150 worth of products.

At the close of the show she told me the apartment manager wanted a Day Radiance and she would go with me to meet her. When we walked into the apartment manager's office, she said, "If you will stay, my assistant wants some Mary Kay also. She will be back in a few minutes."

We started talking, as all women do, and in walked a young man on business with the apartment manager. She introduced me and said, "Mary is a Mary Kay consultant." He exclaimed in loud tones, "Mary Kay? Could I have a Mr. K show?" I replied quickly, "Certainly." I booked a Mr. K show with him for the next day. By this time, the assistant had arrived. I gave her a facial, and sold her a complete set. I went back the next day and held the young man's show. I had sales of $134 there and as soon as I walked into my home after the show, the young man's secretary came by and bought two completes. The next Sunday afternoon the boy who had placed his name in the facial box came by to buy a supply for a relative to take to Venezuela.

I counted $460 sales from that one name in the facial box and the ones who bought have been buying through the years since.

Another experience I had with another facial box concerns one I placed also at another service station.

There the men started kidding each other and one man put his name in the box. When I called his wife, she came to my home. I gave her a facial and she recruited and was my top consultant in my unit for eight years!

There are some rules, however, to be observed when placing facial boxes. I have found if you will offer a prize by drawing and let the person who is in charge of the business do the drawing at the end of the week, it works better. I always just leave the box in one place for one week. You do better if you sell the person in charge on what you are doing.

I had one laundry near my home that kept me busy full time with names from my facial box that I had placed in the laundry. And I always gave away lotions to the management for being so nice to let me place the box there.

When I call to book the facials, I always tell them if they will bring two or three with them, I will give them a nice gift. I always give them a lotion. And I usually have enough for a show each time in my home where everything is handy and I don't have to leave the house.

I have three ways I sell: 1. for cash in full, 2. half the amount and ask them to pay the remainder in two weeks, or 3. I take a post-dated check. By doing this I just sell about every person I give a facial to. If I do have anyone who pays half, then should I lose the rest, I have not made anything but neither have I lost anything because we get our product at half of cost.

I have been in Mary Kay over fourteen years and have never bought less than the minimum in order to make that fifty percent. I am a firm believer in buying so you can make the most profit.

I have one other suggestion on facial boxes. This is something I neglected for so long. If you go out to dinner, take along a facial box and place it in the ladies' room. Then pick it up when you leave and sometimes you get enough for a complete show in just that short time.

Santa Sales

The time to start your Christmas sales is September.
Making preparations, organizing, and getting your attitude girded up are all part of the start-up. The Bible tells us to gird up our mind. We do have the power, you know.

Buy your Christmas wrapping paper in large rolls to save money, wholesale, for women and men both. Then buy a few small rolls of different colors for variety. You will need ribbon, too.

Now place your order for lots of product—remember you can't sell what you don't have, Christmas or anytime. I learned early in my Mary Kay career the hard way. I needed an eye liner brush and drove all the way across town to get one. If I had been a cussing person, I would have cussed myself all the way there and back for being so stupid. I did say, "Now this is for the birds!" So, never again did I borrow.

Buy the miniature bubble bath, Mr. K lotion, and the ladies' lotion. Fix up these in small gifts along with the brushes. These make really nice, inexpensive gifts. Be sure to order plenty of ReVeur After Shave and Mr. K cologne—don't say you can't sell it, because you can.

Our gift sets are a great way to wrap up lots of sales. Order plenty of them—don't be afraid to buy all you possibly can. If you should not sell all you have at Christmas, remember Valentine's Day is just around the corner. People are going to buy something and we have the best and the most reasonable. Order lots of gold purses, travel cases—like 50 to 100 per lots.

Now you have everything ready—organize yourself.
Get yourself a basket loosely woven so packages will show. Weave Christmas ribbon through the basket.

Coke bottle cartons are beautiful sprayed hot pink and wrapped with Christmas ribbon. Excellent for lotions, men's lotions, colognes, bath jell, oil, etc. Wrap one item with Christmas paper and leave one unwrapped so people can see what they look like. Carry these along with the miniature gifts in your beautiful Christmas basket as you deliver. By the way, I wrap while I watch my favorite TV program. You may say, "Oh, you don't make much off this deal." Let me tell you I have made fifty dollars many days off minies alone. The cost is fifty cents for two. You sell them for $1.50 or $1.75. If you sell fifty, that's a very nice profit. Many people will buy ten to twenty per person to use as stocking stuffers.

I start with these in October. When I stop to get my gas tank filled, I show my gifts. When I go to the bank, post office, drive-ins, and you wouldn't believe how many hamburgers I eat during Christmas. I decorate my house Thanksgiving.

The very next day after Thanksgiving, I send out letters to all my customers and put an announcement in the paper to say that I am having Open House to show my Christmas gifts. I set up tables all over the house. Then I wrap one item and set it beside one that is not wrapped. These tables stay up until the day after Christmas. Most of my customer pick up their orders. I finally learned how to train them. When they call for an order or we call them and ask if they need anything, we then say, "Do you want to pick this up or do you want us to deliver it?" This lets them know I will deliver. Many times they say, "I will be in your part of town." Then they pick up their orders. When they come in, I take them around the different tables explaining that we have what they need for everyone. They usually leave with their arms full. If they don't have the money, I take their order, wrap it, and hold it until they are ready for it. I always wrap free.

If my people slow down about coming in and I think of someone who has not bought a gift yet, I call and say, "By the way, Jane, I haven't seen you come by to get your Christmas gift yet. You do want to come before the supply is limited, don't you?" She usually says, "I will be by tomorrow or Saturday." Should she get busy and fail to come, I call again. Remember people are terribly busy around Christmas and they will buy the first thing that they can grab. You only have to show them and tell them what they need. The telephone people have bought for two years $39 minies and thirty to to forty bottles of lotion for their girls for Christmas.

I also set up a table in the Savings and Loan, banks, and any place they will allow me at noon so their employees can buy their gifts. Many of them cannot get out of these places to shop and they are grateful to have someone bring the things they can buy. I sell to automobile sales places, garages, grocery stores, dress shops, and any place I find people.

When a salesperson helps me, I say, "Honey, you have been so nice to me, I want to give you absolutely free a Mary Kay facial and I have lovely Christmas packages I wrap free. Take this folder and make your selection and I will hold it for you until you can pick it up."

I go to different companies I do business with and show them what I have for Christmas gifts and ask them what they usually pay for the employees' gifts. I then select different items that will fit their budget and show them what I have and tell them I will wrap it up, deliver free and if they buy a large order, I usually discount the order some.

One of my insurance friends has bought his Christmas gifts from me for years.

This is the way I get Christmas sales.

The secret is to *start early!*

CHAPTER IX

MANAGING THROUGH PRACTICAL STRATEGIES

Inventory Management

Now that you are a Mary Kay consultant, you have a great responsibility. You must keep a big stock. Stop and give some thought to your responsibility.

You sold that customer. You went to a great deal of trouble to get that customer. You took your time to book her. You used your gas to go to her home. You used your product to give her that facial. You told her Mary Kay was the best company in the world, that the product was special. And it is. You told her we stood behind our commitments and we do. You profiled her and programmed her. You sold yourself to her. Then you go home and the next day you get this call from her saying she would like to buy that perfume you showed her, the one you put on her right arm—oh, yes, the Angel Fire. Could you deliver after noon? Your heart sinks because you know you don't have an Angel Fire because you didn't order enough.

So you run to the phone and call Jane and ask to borrow one. But she doesn't have one. You think, "Oh, I know Mary will have one." You call Mary and she says, "I am so sorry, but I don't have one either." Then you call two or three more consultants and they are out also. Now you have nowhere to go. What will you do?

The only thing left to do is call her back and apologize and tell her she will have to wait. And, oh, dear, you think to yourself, "I can't order now because I don't have the money yet to order." So you wait maybe two weeks before you feel you can order and then you wait for your order from Dallas. But what if the orders are backed up in our warehouse and you have to wait ten days to get your order. When you rush over to deliver your Angel Fire cologne, you are over three weeks late!

Now, think about how your customer feels. If she is like me, she wanted that cologne yesterday before she called you. Then she thinks, maybe this Mary Kay company is not as great as I thought it was. And her estimation of you and your business goes down a few points.

The greatest complaint on our product is that it takes so long to get it because the consultant didn't have it in stock.

I promised myself right away that I would never be without any item, and I've kept that promise to myself. You owe it to your customers to keep stock. Always tell yourself you cannot sell something you do not have. The time spent going after a product could have been spent booking shows.

I remember so well Pope McDonald, our national sales director. Bless his sweet heart. He would say over and over to us directors in Dallas for our week of training, "Now, girls, remember you don't open a store with only a can of tomatoes." I know so well now what he is trying to get us to see.

Let's face it, if you carry a big stock, you are going to have to order big orders. The greatest failure I have experienced with our consultants is they don't order enough products to have for all their sales.

Let's talk about ordering. When you recruit a consultant, try to get her to order at least $500 wholesale.

Show her that if she has her five shows booked, she will be ready to place that $500. Now a word of warning: Don't be too quick to believe them when they tell you they don't have the money.

One time I was recruiting a consultant and she told me she would have to borrow the money and I arranged to go to the bank with her to borrow it. Then the banker whispered to me and said, "Mary, I will loan her the money, but she has $1,500 in her checking account." She placed the $500 order out of the checking account. If they have to borrow the money, show them how they can set it up and pay it off by selling one complete set to make that payment. Many banks would much rather loan $500 than $250.

If she does not have the credit at the bank to borrow the money and has a car, T.V., or furniture, she can go to a finance company and borrow the money.

I very seldom recruit a consultant without a minimum order. Your next step with that consultant is to instruct her not to sell her product and then use any of the money until she has at least three orders placed. I have found my consultants' biggest problem is spending themselves out of business. A consultant is in business for herself, and it is a big business; therefore, it should be run like business. You have to have products to sell or you are out of business.

I always present each new recruit with a specific letter. I keep some printed and on hand for every girl so she will know just what to do. This is a copy of the letter:

As your business consultant, I suggest that you follow this procedure in the McDowell Unit this year as you start your new year.

1. If you have not done so already, open a special account for your Mary Kay business alone.

2. Pay everything having to do with your Mary Kay business by check and get a cash receipt.

3. Pay all meal tickets by check that you can. Keep a paid ticket for all meals.

4. Put every penny of your Mary Kay money in your Mary Kay account. *Never* keep out any cash. If you do, you are sure to spend it.

5. When you take products from your stock for your personal use or for gifts, be sure to make out a pink ticket for it.

6. Never borrow from another consultant and never let stock out of your hands unless you receive payment in full for it.

7. If you mail an order, never wait more than four weeks for your check. Go get it!

8. We suggest you never use your Mary Kay profits when you first start until you have ordered three $500 orders. You got by before you started. Be sure to do so until you get three orders sold.

9. We strongly suggest you never order less than $500 wholesale. If you do, you are not showing yourself that you are a good business woman. This is only enough products to last one good week anyhow!

10. Never let one day go by without setting a goal.

11. Keep all your sales by days, weeks, and months. At the close of each day, check and see if you have reached your goal. If not, write a circle around the amount you have not reached and reach it the next day. Do the same for weeks and months. Watch with joy as your sales climb. Concentrate on your goals and yourself. You will find you will have to eliminate many non-essentials.

12. Each week count your new customers. Write them down in your date book. Determine to get closer to them, to serve them better. Thank God for them. They are your business, you know.

13. Order $500 orders. Win a prize every month.

Look at them even if you don't care for the prize. Win it! Show yourself you can. Ask God to help. Remember, we have minds that will expand and we have never used but a small part of our minds. Let's use them and go to the top. What the mind can conceive, you can receive. Remember, it all starts with you.

You have a responsibility, but your responsibility will bring you such rich rewards. The association with your customers will give you an opportunity to witness for your Lord, an opportunity to become a better mother, a prettier person. Your consultants will be a great deal like you. If you are honest, upright, and pure, they will try to emulate you.

I have tried desperately to emulate Mary Kay. In so doing, I have become a better person. Many times I have been confronted with some situation in which I wondered what to do. I would ask myself, "What would Mary Kay do?" Your consultant will do the same.

We are responsible for ourselves. Our Heavenly Father was so good to allow us to be born, to give us life even before we entered this world. He set before us choices. He gave us the opportunity of choosing how we wanted our life to be. The right choices will force us into success, the wrong choices will lead us to failure.

It is up to us. We are in the driver's seat. If we choose to pay our bills, to be honest and upright and succeed, we can. May we never feel that anyone has kept us from being a success. Let us not say, "I would have done thus and thus if such and such had not happened." When we say this, we sound ridiculous to those who know better.

The first step in the right direction is to acknowledge that if we are a failure, it is only our fault and no one else's. Not only do we have the choice of being a happy, successful person in this life but our Father has arranged for us to have a beautiful home throughout eternity. This depends on you and you alone. You have that choice and should be glad.

The Bible teaches us that if we will accept Jesus, God's Son, and His plan of salvation, we will have a home with Him for eternity.

So you see the right choices will give you everything you need in this life and in the life to come. What kind of choices are you making? Stop and think. Use your mind. Measure up to your responsibilities and make the right choices. There is no excuse for failure.

Remember always your customers are your source of income—be good to them, service them well.

Never complain if you have to deliver a pencil or a rouge. Keep in mind that she or he is your customer and you will sell to them another time. I always make sure that my customers remember me. The reason for this is that so many times I have asked, "Do you use Mary Kay?" They might say "Yes." Then I ask, "Who is your consultant?" And many, many times they say, "I don't know." I always share something with them that will help them remember me. It might be china painting, sewing, growing flowers, canning, cooking, or church. When I part with my customer, I always know she will never forget who I am. I also use labels on my products.

When my customer has a birthday I mail a card, one I have had printed. When her picture appears in the paper or any write-up about her, I mail a card saying, "I saw you in the news." When I see she has been elected an officer in the PTA or any organization, I mail a congratulation card. At Christmas I mail a Christmas card.

We are told that we keep eighty percent of our customers. I have also been told I keep a much higher percentage of my customers than eighty percent simply because I tie them on to me.

I keep a monthly record of my customers and compete with myself each month in trying to have more new customers each month. Many of my dearest friends are my customers. Don't ever neglect them. I also call my customers every two weeks. I approach them in different ways. I might say, "Sally, I just called to tell you we have a new product and I felt sure you would want it." Most often she says she does. The next two weeks I might say, "Sally, I just happened to think. I don't believe you have tried our hand cream." In the next two weeks I might say, "Sally, I just called to see if you liked the shampoo sample I gave you." We sell about every two weeks to our customers in this way.

Time Management

I learned very soon after getting in Mary Kay that I had to watch my time. My neighbors mean much to me and my greatest pleasure is having a cup of coffee with them. The next most pleasant social event in my life is teas. I just love going to teas and showers.

All of a sudden I realized I had to get myself organized if I wanted to sell Mary Kay. I had to start making other arrangements. What I was doing would have to change or else I should quit my career.

I came up with some of these plans:

1. I would arise at six o'clock, dress, have breakfast, get ready by eight to go to work. I would imagine Mary Kay walking in and I wanted to be dressed so she would approve of me. As a consultant up to this time, I didn't dress until near noon.

2. I would get on that phone and book shows for one hour. My best hour, I remember, was booking eight o'clock shows.

3. I learned to answer the phone in a hurried tone, and to make my phone calls very short.

4. I sent gifts to showers but didn't go in person.

5. I excused myself from teas, saying that my schedule was just too heavy. I said I was in business now, and I found my friends loved me just as much. In fact, I think they respected me more for caring for my business.

6. The morning coffees had to go. I explained that I had a show at ten a.m. and had to rush. I asked to be excused.

7. Funerals were another event which I had to make adjustments. I knew just about everyone and it seemed that someone died just about every day. I had to limit my attendance at these.

8. I read my Bible every morning, regardless, and asked God to help me with my business.

9. I read my manual more instead of watching TV. I played motivation tapes or read a motivation book.

10. I set goals—short term and long term goals.

11. I made posters with my goals on them and lined my bedroom with these. They would remind me daily that I had to stay within a limited amount of time more than anything.

During these early years, my weekly goal was $500 per week. My month goal was $1,000 clear each month. At this time I was doing everything myself—shows, delivery, going to the post office and bank, doing my own housework, gardening and sewing. So to sell $500 each week, I had to really plan.

I soon learned to take God as my unseen Partner. He became more real to me each day. I learned He would help me work more efficiently. I made it a habit to lay out my goal before Him, and I want to give Him credit for all my accomplishments.

I disciplined myself not to put off until tomorrow what I could do today. I learned something in grade school that has stayed with me through the years. It goes like this:

> When a task is once begun,
> Never leave it 'til it's done.
> Be the labor great or small,
> Do it well or not at all.

I would repeat these lines over and over again while working.

I made myself like what I was doing and in this way it didn't become a drudgery. Never, never did I allow myself to say, "I hate to do this . . . or that." I made myself attack every problem with great faith that it could be worked out, and I found that it would work itself out. It *always* did.

I believe to be successful is to evaluate yourself. I suggest the following checklist for self-management:

1. Was my appearance that of a professional Beauty Consultant?

2. How many times did I read the Manual before my first week?

3. Did I read my Manual on Show Procedure, Booking, and Coaching before my shows?

4. How may shows did I hold my first week?

5. Did my show postpone? Why?

6. Do I believe the Hide Tanner's Story?

7. Did I tell the Hike Tanner's Story as stated in the Manual?

8. Did I give the Booking talk in the opening remarks?

9. Did I give a Recruiting talk in the opening remarks (or during the show)?

10. Was my hostess sold on the product?

11. Did I kitchen-coach the hostess?

12. How did I put my guests at ease?

13. Did I project my enthusiasm and belief in the product?

14. Did I sell positively, assuming from the beginning that everyone would take Mary Kay home with them?

15. Did I sell mostly Complete, Basic, or Extras?

16. Did I give a definite close and ask for the order, Complete or Basic?

17. Did I help each guest individually with her order?

18. Did I receive objections of why not to buy?

19. Did I receive objections of why not to book?

20. Did I have an answer in the Manual?

21. Was I empathetic or sympathetic?

22. Was my show informative, yet relaxed and fun?

23. Did I book at least two from my show?

24. Did I use the Booking talk in the Manual?

25. Did I mentally select the two I want to book?

26. Did I coach after booking each new hostess as stated in the Manual?

27. Did I book for next week?

The success of a consultant in our business can be accurately gauged by what your hostesses and customers think of you! If they think you are wonderful—then you are! Your business is to WIN FRIENDS AND INFLUENCE PEOPLE!

HOW can you accomplish this?

1. BE THE KIND OF PERSON your hostess would be proud to introduce to her friends!

    a. Dress well—look successful!

    b. Be diplomatic, courteous, tactful, and above all, be sincere!

    c. Remember you are a guest in your hostess's home; behave as if you were the guest of the president's wife.

2. PLAN YOUR SHOW—so that you know what you are going to do—first, last, and always. Make it fast-moving and interesting!

3. REMEMBER it is better that you miss a sale than to sell a woman something that you know is not right for her!

4. IN BOOKING, use the complimentary "booking approach" that flatters them: "At every show I select two or three people that I would most like to have for my future hostesses, and today I have selected YOU. Is there any reason why you couldn't have a show? I think you'd be wonderful!

5. In helping your hostess select her hostess gift, give her EVERY ADVANTAGE you can.

6. Whatever you do, KEEP YOUR PROMISES. Elephants just don't have any memory at all compared to hostesses!

So to sum it up, get your mind off what *you* are going to get out of the Show—for then, and only then, will you be successful! Remember that the people should be getting their "time's worth" at a show as well as their "money's worth." Never forget a customer, and *never let a customer forget you! A few important tips to observe:*

You must be willing to pay a price for success. What is that price?

1. Willing to learn. Attend sales meetings and every workshop possible.

2. Study your manual; it contains twenty-five years of Mary Kay's experience.

3. Be keenly aware of every opportunity.

4. Organize your time.

5. Look like a professional every minute in dress and conduct.

6. Have the right attitude.

7. Debug yourself of the many things that might hinder you.

8. Read some each day on motivating material.

9. ASK GOD TO HELP YOU!

Appointment Management

Never allow a show to cancel until you have really done everything you can to make it hold.

One time I had a show with our church's educational director's wife as the hostess and a deacon's wife from the church board booked a show. This was another time I had not coached the hostess.

The day before the show, my new hostess called me and these were her words: "Mary, I can't have that show, I can't get anyone to come." I said in slow earth-shaking tones, "You don't mean it!" The sound of my voice was as if the thunder had struck the family.

Then I said slowly, "Well, if you can't, you can't. I will just let Mary pay me my hostess credit back." Now I knew she would never, never let me have Mary Kay pay back the hostess credit. She was silent a minute and said, "Well, I will try and see who I can get if you have to do that." I then told her to try very hard to get as many as four. When I arrived for the show, she had four people there. I sold $134 worth of products, and during the show, one lady said, "Mary, what do you have to do to sell this product?" I arranged an appointment with her and recruited her. In turn she recruited her sister-in-law in California. Her sister recruited her sister and I have this sister as an offspring Director with a large unit. Only this week, I had a call from one of her unit members informing me she was placing her letter of intent today. So you see, it pays to do everything we can to keep a show from cancelling.

I have always found it a good policy to pay hostess

credit at the time of the show and handle it in this manner!

1. *Pay the hostess gift in advance.*

In doing this, it is necessary to teach a new consultant to come to an understanding with the hostess at the time the percentage on her show is being figured. This way you almost never lose a show because the hostess feels obligated to you. For instance she has a $100 show with two bookings which equals twenty dollars of hostess percentage. Explain that from the company's standpoint, she cannot receive the gift until her bookings are held. This always gets a sigh of regret. Then say, "I'll tell you what; there is one way you can have your gift today (assuming you *are* delivering at the show!). Tell me, are you pretty sure that Mary or Jane will each *hold* their shows? Are they pretty reliable? If something should happen to one of them, could you find someone to take her place? You see, I will guarantee these shows to the company in order to pay your gift in *advance*; and if something happened that the shows didn't go on, I would be in trouble with the company. Would you be willing to do this?" If the understanding is reached in advance, and the hostess really understands her obligation to you, she will seldom go back on her word!

2. *Definite date — career basis*

Say to your prospective hostess whose date you have just set, "Mrs. Jones, just one thing: You know some of the Mary Kay consultants do this as a hobby; but with me, it's a career! When I set aside a time for you, that means that I will be there, rain or shine, sleet or snow; and, of course, if you should call me the night before and tell me *not* to come, it's like having your husband's company call him and tell him not to come to work tomorrow. So if something should happen that you can't keep your date with me, would you do your best to get someone to take over for you? And if something should happen to me, I will do the same. I'll see you on the 17th. Thank you!

3. *Hostess gift of the week*

Offering a gift to the High Hostess of your week (in addition to the regular percentage) enables you to book for NEXT WEEK. It is a known fact that the sooner a booking is held, the fewer the chances of a postponement. Also, the hostess felt she MUST have the show "next week" because this is a SPECIAL week and the ONLY time she can compete for the extra gift. Besides all this, it very definitely encourages higher sales because the hostess is given until Saturday morning to get in all the extra sales she can to compete with the other four or so hostesses. And is there a woman who doesn't think she can beat any four or five women alive? It's a much different thing than competing with everyone in a city, for example. And remember: just eighteen dollars' worth of retail sales called in earns enough *profit* for you to pay for the gift.

4. *Handling postponements and cancellations*

Never let a show get off your Date Book! When a hostess calls to postpone a show, she often gives you the reason and then says, "I'll call you when I can have it." Remember to be gracious and sympathetic about her reasons for postponing; BUT THEN SAY, "I know you want Mrs. Former Hostess to receive her credit on your shows; and we can do that if another—even tentative—date is set. If it goes off the books, Mrs. Former Hostess loses her credit; and I know you don't want that to happen. So suppose we put down something you think will work, say Tuesday two weeks from now. That way Mrs. Former Hostess won't lose her credit. O.K.?" Always explain that her show has already gone into the company on Mrs. Former Hostess's report; and if that is cancelled outright she loses her credit; but the company will gladly set the date forward!

5. *What to do on cancellations after the gift paid in advance*

If the prospective hostess INSISTS that she cannot set another date and actually cancels, IMMEDIATELY call the former hostess and say, "Mrs. Jones, Mrs. Smith just called and told me that she finds it impossible to have her show, and cancelled. I'm so sorry because it affects your percentage. You remember we discussed that the day of your show when you selected your gift. Can you think of someone we might be able to get to replace her?" Many times, to keep her percentage intact, she will book another show herself, inviting those who didn't get to attend her other show; or she will call around to some of her friends who might have one themselves. Be sure to remind her of these possibilities and seldom, if it is handled right, will you have an actual cancellation!

Another problem facing consultants is "Avoiding Postponements." First of all, an ounce of prevention is worth a pound of cure. Deal with postponements in *advance*—don't wait for them to happen. Some things that will help are:

1. *Learn to book for next week only.* Do not ask a hostess when she would like to have her show. It's a natural tendency for us to put things off for as long as possible. If you allow it, the hostess will book three or four weeks away. However, there is a way to avoid this. First of all, have a full date book—doctor appointments, hair appointments, birthdays, etc.—in other words, your date book should look very BUSY. Ask the hostess, "Which will work better for you, the first of the week or the latter part?" Then when she answers, say, "Tuesday or Wednesday?" Then, "afternoon or

evening?" Give her choices. While looking at your appointment book say, "Let's see when I can do your show." Make her feel you have only a couple of times and that you will work her in—get the idea? "Let's see, I have an opening Tuesday evening; will that work for you?" Please notice: *a specific date has never been mentioned.* Write her name in on that date and say, "Okay, that will be Tuesday, June 4th at 7:30" which is next week, but you never said anything about her show being next week. When you coach her you can then say, "O.K., I'll see you next Tuesday at 7:30." BELIEVE ME, THIS WORKS. And, remember, just how long does someone need to plan their show? One of our problems is that we give people too long and they worry about it . . . it becomes a chore instead of a pleasure.

2. *Overbook.* If you want five shows for next week and you have exactly five on your books, the first thought that will come to your mind on Monday morning is, "Oh, I hope none of my shows postpone." However, if you have ten, and you need only five, the thought of postponements never enters your mind because you know you could afford to lose a few and still have plenty. How many times have you thought, "I just know that show is going to postpone" and then shortly afterward, the phone rings and sure enough it is your hostess doing exactly what you expected her to do. If you do not expect postponements, they will be minimal.

3. *Hostess contest for next week.* Mary Kay says she never went a week without having a hostess contest for "next week." Then, if the hostess wants to book two weeks away, you can say, "Oh, I wish you could have it next week when I'm giving the most away." She will . . .

CHAPTER X

MANAGING THROUGH ORGANIZATION

Office Management

Your office is a very important part of your business. You should keep it organized.

A business in a box is really a must. Loose-leaf binders are so good to have. I have four file cabinets. Everything that comes from the home office is filed in my file cabinets and has been through the years. The fifteen seminars I have attended, the fourteen Jamborees I have attended, all the speeches made by different directors through the years; all applauses are kept and filed including all IBM reports and seminar brochures.

Just this year I devised a plan whereby I can find anything I want beginning January 1. I have a shelf over my desk with loose leaf binders, one each for applause, pending IBM orders, directors memo's, personal orders. All these have large letters printed with a felt pen. I do this so I can get anything I want at once.

My customers are called every two weeks. My secretary calls my pink tickets, delivers my product, and books my shows, goes to the bank and post office, and reconciles my bank accounts. I have a part-time secretary who types additional letters. This leaves me free to recruit, train, sell, and promote. I have a maid one day each week.

After so many years of trying to do everything myself, I learned it was more profitable to have extra help and sell products and pay for the help.

We use the mail freely to communicate with consultants and directors. This requires many letters going out.

Most of my printing is done at the printers. I do have a good copy machine, two typewriters that I won from Mary Kay, two adding machines, and three desks. One of my desks is in my bedroom by my bed. When I think of some idea to help my business, I get out of bed and write it down. Many times I get up at two or three o'clock and compose a letter to my consultants.

I have an office, a product room, conference room, and an interview and meeting room. My meeting room is 14 × 30 feet and is used for meetings only. Early in my career I bought folding and card tables, couches and chairs. I have seven of these. Meeting places are hard to find in my town and my girls like coming to my home much better. My conference room is equipped like a living room. My interviewing room serves as a dining room. I own a movie machine and own all the company tapes. These have proven very valuable tools in getting across my message to recruits and prospective recruits alike.

I would certainly advise any consultant who wants to become a director to purchase a movie outfit at once. I have a teenager who puts on labels for me.

Every beauty book, order cards, and any other paper materials should have your label on it. Hundreds of times I have asked, "Who sells you your product?" I don't want to take someone else's customer if they are caring for them. All too often I have received this answer, "I really don't know who it was I bought from."

I am a great believer in letting your customer have more than one address of yours.

Never let your papers get piled up on your desk. You are sure to lose something valuable if you do. Handle papers only once. I like to get up early and get all correspondence and paper work done before eight o'clock. This allows me time to dress and be ready to start my day's work.

Never have I been able to figure out how anyone can be a success in Mary Kay and sleep late every morning. I can't and I don't believe anyone else can. The best plan I know is to get up at six o'clock. This will give you one hour for your paper work and one hour to have breakfast and dress before beginning your business day.

Reports

I like for every girl to know when she turns in her letter of intent that her summary sheets will go in with the letter. Without her reports, I have no way of helping her.

When I look at her reports and find that she has not sold well, I can teach her more about the product. If she has sold and not booked, this tells me she does not know her booking techniques and I can teach her more on how to book. Maybe she sells and books but doesn't recruit. When I look at her reports, I can see she does not know her recruiting. But without the reports, it is impossible to help the consultant as much. Reports are very important to you and your director.

Here is a report that I suggest to my consultants:

1. The first thing to do when filling out this report is to put your name on it and your consultant number!

2. Enter the date—Your weekend (Saturday). This is a company policy and it is important that we all do it alike.

3. Enter shows only—A show must consist of at least three people receiving facials. Any sales other than show sales go into "telephone sales" column; this includes private and double facials!

4. All sales shown on your Weekly Report are *sales only*—no tax. Check your columns and if you have any odd cents showing anywhere, you know you are adding in tax. A good rule of thumb where hostesses are working for their Skin Care is—Report all cash in only!

5. Enter your wholesale order only if you have sent it in. Enter it *only once*. Enter total of Section One wholesale only. Mail a copy of this order to me at the same time you mail your order to Dallas. *It is very important that I have a copy of this order as soon as you mail it to the company.*

6. Send in a Weekly Report *every week*. Even if you had a zero week fill in the back side of it also.

7. Local consultants should bring their reports to sales meetings or mail them on Saturday so that they will arrive by Monday. Out of town consultants should mail their reports on Saturday so that they arrive by Monday—airmail! If your weekly report is late getting to me, then my reports are late. Also, you do not get the recognition you deserve in your unit newsletters! Should you decide to take a step up to Directorship, this would suddenly become a crisis in your life and mine! You absolutely would not be accepted for Directorship training without these! To go back and do six months at one time is hard!

8. Send in the white copy of the sales ticket with

your report. Mark "R.O." on those sales that are re-orders.

I wonder if you've ever stopped to realize how vitally important an accurate Weekly Summary to your Director can be to YOU? With it she can diagnose any "ILL" you might be suffering in your career.

Below is an example of one consultant summary for the month and what was revealed. This particular consultant began as a career girl, that is to say, she held a job elsewhere, and worked part-time at her Mary Kay job. Within a short time she found herself making more per hour with Mary Kay, Inc. than at her other job. She decided to go full-time with Mary Kay. It happens that she was a divorcee with a small child to support. She felt that would enable her to be with her child more of the time. By holding only seven shows a week, with her average she could equal the amount she was presently making on both jobs—all in just twenty-one hours a week as opposed to forty hours she was presently putting in.

So she switched and this came to our attention when after a month or so she found herself unable to book or hold more than approximately four shows a week—which was insufficient for her needs. She said, "I just can't book enough." Her director went over her booking techniques with her and found she knew how to "cold book." So obviously booking was actually the "fever" that indicated something else was wrong.

Her summary is listed in Table I.

From this report her director was able to uncover and correct the following "ills";

1. 3.4 guests per show indicated that she was not coaching her prospective hostess. Booking .81 from 3.44 guests was booking about one out of four which was

INDIVIDUAL CONSULTANT SUMMARIES

Week	Shows	Attended	Booked	Show Sales	Telephone Sales	Total Sales	Attended Sales Meetings
1	4	14	3	$150.00	$ 9.97	$159.97	Yes
2	4	16	4	200.00	8.00	208.00	No
3	5	15	4	225.00	5.00	230.00	Yes
4	3	10	2	100.00	2.00	102.00	No
Total	16	55	13	$675.00	$ 24.97	$599.97	
Average	4	3.4	4.81	42.18	6.24	139.75	

Table I

fine. She was taught to "coach" and by increasing her attendance to six guests, she began averaging two bookings per show.

2. With six guests instead of 3.44, her sales automatically doubled and she found herself selling $84 per show instead of $42.

3. The second *ill* discovered was that she wasn't calling pink tickets. (Formerly working 49 hours a week, she simply hadn't had time to do this and when she switched to full time, she had failed to realize its importance. Spending one hour a day calling "pink tickets," she increased her phone sale from $6.24 weekly to an average of $100 per week.

4. The third *ill* discovered was she hadn't gotten in the habit of attending sales meetings when she was a career girl, and failed to realize that this is where we as consultants recharge our batteries weekly by exchanging ideas and being inspired to do what others are doing. Regular attendance at sales meetings soon brought her increased earnings.

5. The fourth *ill* was that she was failing to order efficiently as she might have. By placing $250 orders at fifty percent commission she increased her earnings con-

siderably over ordering $100 lots and saved all the freight costs!

This all ads up to almost a "Cinderella Story" of a consultant's success. It can be your story, too!

Creative Coaching

A show worth having is worth coaching.

This is one place in my career where I almost failed. Somehow I didn't learn to coach my hostesses properly and when I would book a show—which I had no trouble doing—I would not follow through with it. Early in my career I would book a show and when I arrived, many times they would not be home.

One day I booked a show with a lovely girl. After making three trips to her office, I did not call her or coach her at all. When the time came, I arrived at her apartment with all my products and case. This was during the time when we carried so much it looked like we were moving in when we arrived. Finally I found her apartment on the second floor. After carrying all that paraphernalia up the steps on a very hot day, I knocked on her door. A beautiful girl opened the door and I asked to see my hostess. The girl replied that my hostess was babysitting that day at a lady's home.

You can guess my frustrations. I was plain mad. In fact, I was furious. All my show materials were then carried back down the long flight of stairs. When I returned home, it suddenly dawned on me. It was not that girl's fault at all. It was mine and mine alone. I had not coached her at all.

From that day forward I always coached my hostesses just like the manual tells us to. Let me remind you here: That manual will give you step for step how to do your Mary Kay business; if we neglect to follow, we will have to suffer the pain of neglect.

Have respect for that manual. It has twenty-five years of Mary Kay experiences within its pages.

Please don't neglect to coach your hostess.

You should have the following objectives in mind when you're coaching each hostess:

1. Motivate and inspire her.
2. Tell her how to invite her guests.
3. Tell her to invite enough guests to have at least six persons present.
4. Tell her how to get bookings from those who couldn't come to her show.
5. Tell her how to have those present ready to Buy and Book.

We suggest you begin to coach your hostess immediately, as soon as the show date is in your datebook.

Give each hostess a "Suggestions for the Hostess" booklet stamped with your name and phone number.

1. Review the booklet with her. It only takes a minute or two. Underline key phrases in the booklet such as . . . "Thank you," "My Career," "Arrive Early," "I'll bring everything with me" (including washcloths), and "Keep refreshments simple."
2. We suggest you also underline, "Two shows will guarantee your full show credits of 20%." Encourage her to have two booking prospects lined up ahead of time. Suggest that she list their names in the spaces provided on the back of the booklet.

Tell her exactly how to invite her guest: "I am having a professional Beauty Consultant coming to my home at 7:30 Thursday evening, (Date I) to show proper skin care and makeup techniques. She is allowing me to invite five guests. I need to know for sure that you are coming, so I can reserve a place for you."

Give the hostess a supply of beauty books, order cards, price lists, and miniature lotions. Stress the importance of her obtaining outside orders. They count towards her show credit. (Have her collect the money and let you know the products ordered so that you can have them with you for delivery to her at the show.)

Coaching "Tips":

1. Have her guests dress casually.
2. Put emphasis on inviting those who have not had a Mary Kay facial.
3. Take orders from those who are using the product. Sell Body Lotion, Glamour, and Mr. K items to those who can't attend.
4. Try to book those who can't come and who haven't had a facial "to guarantee the twenty percent hostess credit."
5. Be on the lookout for anyone who "might like to do what I do." Suggest that she write the names of consultant "candidates" in the space provided on the back of the "suggestion for the hostess" booklet.
6. Finally remind your hostess again that this is a career with you. You probably "won't call" but will just be there 30 minutes before the show is due to begin.

Send Reminder Card on Tuesday of the preceeding week. Add a personal note.

At your show ask the hostess for the "Suggestions" booklet. If she has followed your instructions, you may notice names of girls who weren't at the show. Ask your hostess if she minds if you call them.

CHAPTER XI

SOARING WITH EAGLES

You can be what you want to be! You must first have the desire. If you did not have the ability to do what you want to do, you would not have the desire in the first place. And the person who recruited you knew you could do a good job or she would not have recruited you.

You are probably saying, "Now you may be able to do the things you are doing, but I could never do what you have done." Oh, yes, you can . . . if you have the desire.

The first thing you should do is turn your life over to the Lord Jesus and He will make you the person you would like to be. Allow me to tell you a story out of my experience.

I am a collector of things—antiques, dishes, any kind of dishes, such as Mexican pottery. I like anything artistic.

I have been told that I am very creative. I sew and make things, I paint china and pictures. In fact, just about everything loose, I can turn into something ornamental. For instance, I see things around the house such as egg cartons, coke bottles, bleach bottles, coffee cans. From all of these things I can make something.

One day I decided to make some pottery from clay. I

sought out a good teacher and had her teach me how to take clay and mold with my hands some beautiful things. After they were fired in a kiln and painted, they were beautiful.

One day my teacher taught me how to mold a lady's slipper. She then showed me how to take ordinary heavy cotton lace, put a ruffle around the top of that slipper, then mold the petals and leaves of a rose to be placed on the toe. The slipper was then put in a kiln and fired at a high degree of heat for some time; then taken out and painted. I painted the slipper with white glaze. The roses were given a rose colored glaze and the leaves green.

What joy I had from knowing I had taken ordinary clay and made a thing of such beauty. I have cherished that slipper for several years and money could not buy it, because I made it!

Today as I look at that slipper, I am reminded of what God has done for me. He created us just as I did the slipper. He must want us to have a beautiful life, to stand out in the crowd. He wants us to be the person that people will look at and say, "This is truly a beautiful person. Her life is clean and pretty." He didn't make us to wallow in sin and degradation. We are wonderfully made and we should reflect our appreciation and awe of the Creator, of His power and genius. May we let our lives be clay in the hand of the Master Potter.

You may be going through the fires of life. Disappointments and troubles may at this moment be burning out the dross in your life just as the kiln burns the clay.

Let me tell you, my friend, turn to Jesus, the Master Potter. He can take your life and make something beautiful of it. He made you in the first place and He made you to be happy.

I heard a story one time about an eagle. A man caught

an eagle and chained it to a chopping block in the barn-yard with the chickens, turkeys and geese. One day a man came by and was visiting with the eagle's owner and asked, "Why do you have that eagle chained to that chopping block?" The owner replied, "To keep him from flying away." The visitor then asked him how much he would sell it for. The owner said, "Oh, make me an offer." The visitor said, "Twenty-five dollars." The man replied, "I'll take it." Then the visitor said, "Unchain him." He did. The eagle just stood there, didn't move. About that time, a bird flew overhead. The eagle shook his head two or three times, began to raise his wings, and flew off into the blue sky. Then the man who sold the eagle turned to the other man to ask, "Why did you do that?" Replied the man, "Because an eagle was made for the sky. He was not made to stay down here in the barnyard with the barnyard fowls."

You were made to be a beautiful Christian, fashioned by the Master Potter. You may say, "Oh, but I am like the clay. I could never be like the beautiful slipper, catching everyone's eyes which look my way." Yes, we can all be like that. Just as I put the glaze and added beautiful color in the roses and a white glaze over the slipper, if you will turn your life over to the Master Molder of everything, the Lord Jesus Christ, I promise you He will make you over, change you, and you will be a chosen vessel fashioned by His loving hands and be more beautiful than my pretty slipper.

You can be the top person in Mary Kay if you will turn your life over to Jesus and let Him make you the person you want to be.

Set your goal to be a winner. Plan to be somebody—someone your family and friends will be proud of.

Remember, you have to win your family's and

friends' respect. To do this, you must have a healthy self-image. Your imagination is your world. You must see yourself winning before it happens. You must think like a winner, walk, talk and act every hour in the day like a winner. Napoleon said, "Imagination rules the world." Einstein said, "Ambition is everything." You might imagine with pictures and words and with emotion the role you want to play. It is not what we are that holds us back; it is what we think we are not.

How we feel about ourselves is everything. Dr. Maxwell Maltz, the great plastic surgeon, said the greatest discovery of the century was the self-image. If we think we are not important, we will become unimportant. Another way to say this is that if we think we are failures, we will become failures. Form a mental picture of yourself as a great person.

Imagination, then, is the key word. When we change our self-image our behavior will follow. We must dwell on the person we would like to become. If you are to be a winner, see yourself in the winner's circle. See yourself on that stage. Hear your name called. See Mary Kay coming forward with that big beautiful smile and a beautiful prize in her hand to give to you. Hear the music playing your song. You can be the winner you want to be!

Remember God cares for you.

After a busy day, I sat down to read the evening newspaper. Right on the front page was a report that thousands across the land are starving for lack of food. Further down on the same page was an account of two old people having been robbed and killed. I then turned the page only to encounter a report of a mother being prosecuted for having murdered her child. Things weren't any better a page or two further into the paper. What a wicked world we live in, I thought. It was so sickening that I didn't care to read any more of the paper.

I will go to bed and forget it all, I told myself. But, I was very sadly disappointed, because my mind was so troubled that I could not find solace in sleep. Finally, I did drop off to sleep.

Upon arising Saturday morning, I felt that the whole world was on my shoulders. I just dropped into a chair by the window and looked outside in my back yard. I could see beautiful flowers in bloom. Birds were winging cheerfully in every direction. And, oh, how beautiful they looked without a care in the world. I went outside. The sun was shining so brightly. The cool, crisp air felt so good on my face. All of a sudden I caught a glimpse of a beautiful red robin perched high on the telephone wire singing as though his lungs would burst.

The thought crossed my mind: Why can't I be as happy and free as the bird? And suddenly I seemed to hear the words of Jesus being spoken to me saying, "Cast your burden on me for I care for you." Then I remembered all the responsibilities I had for the day. The car insurance and all of the household bills had to be paid. I started to groan under the load. Again that sweet voice spoke to me tenderly saying, "Look at those flowers out there. They don't work and you will never be as beautiful as they. Don't you hear those birds singing? Your Heavenly Father takes care of them. Don't you know that you are of more value than all of these?"

I turned again to look at the robin, but he was raising himself in flight. I said to myself, "So you are going someplace." Upon reflection, I also said to myself, "I am going to take a journey before too long myself. I have already made the arrangements. I have bought my ticket. I have paid the fare. And you know what, Jesus is coming and He is going to take me by the hand and lead me all the way there. I don't even have to go alone."

I went back into the house with a whole new outlook for the day. The burdens of the world had been lifted. I felt better for I know He cares.

So today if you are depressed, lonely, despondent, stop and take a good look at what you are and what you can become. Remember the Lord is your Shepherd. The 23rd Psalm says it all.

What is the shepherd for? The shepherd stands between the sheep and all danger. The Lord stands by and defends you. He will not let you want. He has made it possible for us to have anything our hearts desire. If we will only reach out and claim it. Believing Him, ask and it shall be given you. He leads us into paths of righteousness for His name's sake. He gives us peace in our souls, the peace that lets you lie down at night and know that all is well. He will make you what you desire to be.

You were made for the higher things of life. If you allow yourself to be shackled with fears, doubts, and negative thinking you can change that at once. All you have to do is turn your eyes to Jesus and ask Him to free you! Believe and trust Him for His Word is true. You are the only voice God has to speak for Him.

There is no need for depression. Find someone who needs you and help that someone. Determine to flap your wings and arise out of that despondent feeling. Arise like that robin in my backyard did from that telephone line and fly to the top in this world. You have the power. It's up to you.

I want to see you happy, joyful, enthusiastic, bright, and shining in this world.

I will see you on stage!

Appendices

I. LETTER SAMPLE TO THOSE WHO DO NOT COME TO SALES MEETINGS

Dear Sally,

I feel so terrible about not being able to provide for you the motivation you need to help you in your career.

I really don't know what to do and I need some response from you. What can I do to earn your respect and your presence at sales meetings? I know you don't do anything worthwhile as long as you are absent from sales meetings. And all the energy and hard work I spend to prepare good meetings for you is wasted unless you attend.

You know and I know that Mary Kay says that if you miss one meeting, you are sick, miss two and you are dying, miss three and you are dead. And I will need to send flowers!

We sure don't want to have to send you flowers. I know how great the Mary Kay life can be. We need you and you need us. All of us together can make it greater. But you or I cannot do it alone.

Can I expect you at the next sales meeting?

I love you,
Mary

II. TEXT OF CONSULTANT'S PLEDGE

Once there was a woman who thought she could take some of the ingredients Jesus used and make a woman whose unblemished life would reflect Jesus Christ.

This woman built the company known as Mary Kay Cosmetics, Inc.

Do you as a representative of Mary Kay promise to attend all meetings, both sales and social? Do you promise to never defame the name of another consultant? Do you promise to deal honestly with your customers and seek at all times to uphold the Mary Kay image?

This light represents Integrity. As you deal with your customers, you must be honest.

This light represents Courage. Courage to keep on when the going gets rough.

This light represents Faith. Faith in God and in yourself.

This light represents Prosperity. You can have anything you want because you have a way to earn the money to pay for it.

This light represents Growth. As you grow in your business, you grow in knowledge.

The light that you all hold depicts the love you have in your heart for God and for your family and for sister consultants.

Wherever you find a sister consultant, do you promise to treat her as a sister?

III. SUGGESTIONS FOR NEW YEAR RESOLUTIONS

As your business consultant, I suggest that you follow this procedure in the McDowell Unit this year as you start your New Year.

1. If you have not done so already, open a special account for your Mary Kay business alone.

2. Pay everything having to do with your Mary Kay Business by check and get a cash receipt.

3. Pay all meal tickets by check that you can. Keep a paid receipt for all meals.

4. Put every penny of your Mary Kay money in your Mary Kay account. *Never* keep out any cash. If you do, you are sure to spend it.

5. When you take products from your stock for your personal use or for gifts, be sure to make out a pink ticket for it.

6. Never borrow from another consultant and never let stock out of your hands unless you receive payment in full for it.

7. If you mail an order, never wait more than four weeks for your check. Go get it!

8. We suggest you never use your Mary Kay profits when you first start, until you have ordered three $500 orders. You got by before you started. Be sure to do so until you get three orders sold.

9. We strongly suggest you never order less than $500 wholesale. If you do, you are not showing yourself that you are a good business women. This is only enough product to last you one good week anyway!

10. Never let one day go by without a *set goal*.

11. Keep all your sales by days, weeks and months. Each day at the close, check and see if you have reached your goal; if not, write a circle around the amount you

have not reached and reach it the next day. Do the same for weeks and months. Watch with joy as your sales climb. Concentrate on your goals and yourself. You will find you will have to eliminate many non-essentials.

12. Each week, count your new customers. Write them down in your date book. Determine to get closer to them—to serve them better. Thank God for them; they are your business, you know.

13. Order $500 Orders: Win a prize every month. Look at them, even if you don't care for the prize. Win it! Show yourself you can. Ask God to help you. Remember we have minds that will expand. We have only used but a small part of our minds. Let's use them this year and go to the Top!

Mary

IV. THE MARKETING PLAN

I took a large poster board 2½ by 3 feet. Down in the right hand corner I drew a large black pot. I got some paper bills from the Chamber of Commerce and pasted them like they were falling out of the pot because it was so full. I called this the Avenues of Income from Mary Kay.

I drew a line with the $68.25 for the case.

The next line for the minimum order and the tax, always explaining that Mary Kay lets us pay the tax and we don't have to bother with reports. I learned early in my recruiting that people hate making tax reports. I don't blame them. I do, too. So I stop this question about it before they have to ask.

The next lines having arrows going into my pot of earnings, are:

1 recruit to 5—4% recruit checks
5th recruit—5% going into the pot
6th recruit—6% going into the pot
7th recruit—7% going into the pot

Eight is the same way. At this point I have ready the Applause Magazine for the month and show them how much money the top 8% club members got for the month.

The next line is when you get 10 recruits. You put your letter of intent in to become a director.

You now have the opportunity to earn up to as much as 12% plus your 8% plus your 50%. I then explain that it does not stop here if someone in your unit wants to become a director also. You will drop 12%, but will get 4%. Then you may get this from everyone in her unit. And when you have so many off-spring, you can become a National Sales Director.

I then show them the Applause Magazine, again

showing what the top nationals are earning for the month.

I then show them the top line, that shows that 80% of their customers will buy again and again.

V. TELEPHONE REMINDERS

Here are four easy steps to follow when inviting your guests to attend your beauty class so they *will* come:

1. Tell them this is NOT A PARTY but rather this is a private skin care class.

2. Let them know that this is on a "Reservation only" basis and that you can only have a limited number of guests (6 to 8 is ideal).

3. Make sure you get a definite answer, because you are reserving a place for her. Let her know that her being there—and on time—is important.

4. Your Mary Kay beauty class is a special event. When your guests realize this, they *won't want to miss it.*